the

JOY

manifesto

Jax Black
Tomer Yogev

the JOY *manifesto*

Detach from the Corporate Mindset.
Access Your Heart.
Lead with Wisdom.

The Joy Manifesto

Detach from the Corporate Mindset. Access Your Heart. Lead with Wisdom.

ISBN 978-1-5445-3292-9 Hardcover

       978-1-5445-3293-6 Paperback

       978-1-5445-3294-3 Ebook

To our chosen family

who gave us the space to breathe into

the wisdom of joy in our hearts.

It is with the utmost grace and gratitude

that we dedicate this book to you.

We send to you all the light and love the

world has to offer for your

continued evolution.

CONTENTS

ACKNOWLEDGMENTS

We'd like to thank each and every one of the wonderful leaders that we've had the privilege of working with on their journeys into joy. To witness the light of each heart turning on with such brilliance is truly what elevated us into the overflow of our own joy. We are forever grateful to those leaders who have chosen this path, without whom we would never have understood the full impact of joy on leadership. This book is for you and for everyone you have impacted on your journey.

We are also called to thank those who poured their light, heart, and genius into the final manifestation of this book. So, to Layla Forrest-White, Bianca Pahl, Alan Gintzler, Skyler Gray, and Natalie Sowa, we thank you, from the bottom of our hearts.

THE JOY MANIFESTO

*Your authentic leadership presence is
embedded in how you have been living and leading
so well, in spite of all the challenges.*

You did not get this far in life by fixing who you are not.

You have gotten here because of who you are.

Your strengths renewed through the wisdom of joy.

*In your authentic leadership presence, you will no
longer need to, or want to, fight "the good fight."*

*Instead, you will see the fight for what it is.
You will step off the battlefields that have led you to
believe your weaknesses, obstacles, and struggles
belong to you or are a part of the path
to becoming a better leader.*

*You will get to where you want to go by being the leader
you are designed to be and always have been.*

Of all the things we obsess over,
so little of it is relevant to our humanity.

We unfairly ask ourselves to advance as
we constrain the very breath that our hearts need,
the breath that allows us to love ourselves and grow,
simply because we want to be, and deserve to
be, more fully expressed in the world.

To all the souls that are reawakening to
their own self-love and inner light, know that
you are whole and always have been.

It is the constraints of big business,
politics, and religion that have made joy
irrelevant to leadership.

Beyond the survival mindset,
know that your joy is relevant to the bottom line
of how you live and lead, and it is necessary
for our collective evolution.

PREFACE

For the past dozen years or so, we have had the great honor of working with leaders at all levels of organizations, big and small. We have served as educators, consultants, interim executives, and coaches across varied corporate and community settings. During that time, we've continually encountered a singular truth: far too many truly authentic leaders are not making their way to leadership positions where they could cultivate a more positive organizational culture and thereby have greater impact on the world.

Instead, many are sitting at the brink of leadership, waiting "until they are ready." At some point along the way, they were taught that they must wait until they look the part, have a certain number of years under their belt, receive recognition, or are otherwise anointed. In fact, many leaders with good hearts, strong values, and accountability are opting out of higher leadership positions because they don't want to compromise themselves. Quality leaders whose teams respect their authenticity are being pushed out of their leadership roles for not having enough "executive presence."

Organizations continue to hire leaders who perform the part well enough to "fit in" but don't know how to lead people effectively. We are therefore experiencing a crisis in leadership that is spiraling out of control. Researchers study leadership behavior, trying to figure out how so many poorly behaving leaders have claimed seats of power, the C-suite, and even the Oval Office. As it turns out, the root cause of this absurdity—promoting people to positions of power for which they are not suited—is the result of too much leadership by brain and not by heart.

A BROKEN MODEL

Thinking our way to the top is dangerous because it centers ego over heart, and power over people. Through our work with leaders of many stripes, including entrepreneurs, community organizers, heads of nonprofits, and Fortune 500 CEOs, it has become clear that this model of leadership is seriously broken. All too often, good leaders feel they are imposters masquerading at the corporate ball. They complain of having to lead in positions that are not aligned with their innate talents and passions. People progress up the ladder of leadership disengaged from any higher cause to serve their companies, clients, stakeholders, or employees.

It is time for a change. We have written this book for your heart, not your brain. If you are in your brain, we invite you back into your heart. Over time, humanity has become overly reliant on our brains. As a result, our minds have become fields of fear, anger, and struggle because our brains, while capable of holding facts and figures, have no foundation to anchor us internally. Brain knowledge is focused on the outside and driven by facts and belief systems that we string together into thoughts. One person's facts and beliefs can be completely different from another's. Both could be right. Both could be wrong.

More importantly, fighting for an entire lifetime over who has the right facts and figures without knowing who we are in our hearts is futile and counterproductive. Brain energy thrives on competition; whoever argues their viewpoint best is the winner, regardless of whether they are, in fact, right or wrong. Success is measured by material wealth and the power to manipulate and control people and ideas. In today's culture, there is no accountability for the ego-driven brain and no appeal to heart and wisdom.

Yet historically, the most successful civilizations—the Mesopotamians, Greeks, Egyptians—centered the heart before the brain. Unfortunately, this wisdom has been lost over time as humanity has striven to the drumbeat of the brain, reaching for modernity and mass production, forgetting the natural rhythm of our hearts.

So we now find ourselves at the crossroads of competition, in a winner-take-all world with far too many losers. For the broad mass of humanity, overreliance on the brain at the expense of the heart isn't working. Too many are in poverty or struggling to make ends meet. The middle-class dream is ever further from reach—unless humanity takes a turn back to its heart.

A NEW MODEL OF LEADERSHIP

In 2009, we stepped into this work with the launch of our coaching and consulting practice, The Big Joy Theory. At the time, we did so hoping to spread a more whole and complete model of leadership that could illuminate the path to what we call "joywork." We combined our individual consulting practices because we felt that everyone deserved a true partner in the journey to becoming their most authentic and brilliant selves. In our first book, *Unlock The Corporate Mindset*, we mapped a path to authenticity in leadership. In this book, we go further to bring readers closer to the inherent value of joy-based leadership.

Together we must drop the illusion that growth and productivity can occur only through competition and struggle. Instead, we need to identify and leverage the wisdom of our hearts in joy within us. By integrating self-love with leadership, we can alter the structures of a corporate mindset that values power and authority above all else.

This new model of leadership is for everyone who has ever thought, "There must be a better way." It's for those who have ever doubted themselves and misjudged their abilities under a harsh, impossible framework entrenched as the only path to success. It's for those who have ever felt that they had to apologize for not walking the straight and narrow all the way up to the corporate suite. And it's for those who have ever had their good intentions weaponized in the workplace.

Many of you, like us, have endured a long, winding journey trying to find your way to effective, growth-oriented leadership. We, like you, have gone through times when it felt like we could only learn from struggle. Exhausted from the journey, our hearts finally said, "Enough. The struggle isn't working." But if we weren't going to fight, what would we do? Our hearts responded by giving us permission to listen, learn, and lead from a place of joy.

As a result, our entire world flipped inside-out and right-side-up. We began to access the data of our own lived experience, much of which we'd forgotten along the way. It was an evolutionary journey into joy, a shift out of our egos and back into the inner brilliance of our own hearts. And now we are calling upon the hearts of every leader to do the same and find their way back to joy.

Humanity can no longer afford the trauma and drama of climbing the old, broken ladder of leadership. It is time to live and lead with real wisdom and profound self-awareness. This book provides a transformative process that will shift the foundation of how you live and lead from that which is outside of you to all that is inside of you, waiting to be rediscovered and leveraged. Through the profound understanding of who you are as a leader, and through the lens of self-love, you will come to know that you are enough and always have been. By centering the wisdom of your heart at the core of how you lead, you will begin to illuminate new ideas, pathways, and opportunities to become the leader you were always meant to be.

As you learn to live and lead from within, you will see just how easy it is to lead authentically. As you vacate the corporate mindset, you'll learn to choose your heart over your brain, using a soul-inspiring leadership model for success.

Brain energy may have served its purpose during the early years of the Industrial Revolution, but heartlessness, sixteen-hour workdays, low pay, and child labor came to rule the day. We've seen major shifts since then, much for the good, but also increasing political and social upheaval in the first decades of the twenty-first century. Our crisis in leadership has come to a head, where the brain resides, so the time has truly come for leadership with heart. This is the work that needs to be done.

In Part I of this book, Detach from the Corporate Mindset, you'll learn to free yourself from the broken yet ubiquitous model of leadership. In Part II, Access Your Heart, you'll center your heart with joy for the work ahead. In Part III, Lead with Wisdom, you will find the transformative power for truly authentic leadership, today and tomorrow.

As you take this journey with us, here are a few markers to keep in mind along the way:

1. We use the term "self-love" frequently in the book to help bring your heart back to the foundation of leadership. Each time you see it, please consider it an invitation to take a deep breath and relax into your heart. As you will come to understand, self-love is the foundation of joy, necessary to reorient ourselves for the journey. This is not a book to be raced through. It is a book to be experienced. So, do not hesitate to take a moment, breathe, and reconnect with your own self-love every time you happen across the term.

2. The journey you are taking is a cyclical one. If you try to find a straight line through it, you will miss the message. Your heart follows the path of nature, which isn't a linear frame. The language of the heart speaks to the cyclical evolution of all things.

3. This journey is a calling home to your heart. It is, in fact, nothing new but something to be remembered, always. Consider this book a reset for your soul. If that means it takes effort or time, simply consider it an indication that you are, in fact, doing the work.

4. A book alone cannot do the work of transformation. Your heart does that. Once centered in your heart, you will be able to process the data of the world more fully and with a new lens. You will see the world more clearly and engage in it from a new perspective, creating a transformative experience.

We genuinely believe that the real and truest answers to the problems people wrestle with lie just under the surface in our very hearts. It is with great love, light, and joy that we endeavor to bring this message to you so you can radiate your own joy as an effective leader in this world. We look forward to sharing this age-old wisdom and partnering with you on your journey into joy.

And so may it be. Let's begin.

In joy,
Jax & Tomer

Part I

DETACH FROM THE CORPORATE MINDSET

Chapter 1

THE COLONIAL MIND

We begin our leadership journey with the intention to emotionally and energetically disconnect from the power-centered mindset that has driven us into our brains and out of our hearts. This brain-driven attachment to the old, broken model of success has kept us climbing the proverbial corporate ladder. To detach from this corporate mindset, we need to reclaim our innate understanding of our own joy: what it is, where it comes from, and how to access it.

When detaching yourself from toxic models of leadership or negative behaviors, it is critical to return to the root. This is where the journey must begin to effectively release your brain from the mechanisms of deficiency and control built into corporate leadership systems. This is often called the "colonial mindset," established by power structures that historically placed people deemed superior over people deemed inferior. In the colonial mindset, joy is either irrelevant to work or it is to be gained through the accumulation of power and wealth. For the colonial mindset, joy is, at best, merely a byproduct of success. It isn't considered relevant to how humans grow and evolve.

To truly engage in joy and unlock its potential for human development, we must shed the colonial mindset and decolonize joy.

In order to decolonize joy, four things must occur:

1. Joy must be reclaimed as something motivated from the inside, not from outside of us.
2. Joy must come innately from the center of each heart; it is not something we must labor for.
3. Joy must shift from an output of success to a productive input that drives our best selves.
4. Joy must be elevated from a privilege to a right.

NAME THE PROBLEM

As the root cause, we must identify and name the colonial mindset. Otherwise, we are unable to detach ourselves from it. For example, a leader whose organization was steeped in drama and trauma once asked, "How do I solve this?" to which we replied, "First, you must be willing to name the problem in full. Because that which hasn't been named maintains its power."

This is why it is vital for people to name for themselves their hurts, their abusers, and the ways that other people have trespassed against their personhood. This is also why we need to name our attachment to the corporate mindset in all its manifestations. Each leader must finally see how, despite their attempts to fight against it, they have been socialized to attach themselves to an external, hierarchical, and fragmented model of success.

> Leadership has less to do with how far up a corporate ladder you can climb, and more to do with how far you can walk in your own soul.

As we will demonstrate throughout this book, the corporate mindset model of success saps our very breath and detaches us from the wisdom in our hearts. This is why leaders are feeling diminished in their work and exhausted in their souls. Leadership has less to do with how far up a corporate ladder you can climb, and more to do with how far you can walk in your own soul.

We start by untangling the web of unspoken rules in the traditional model of success. We each need to recognize and name the ways in which we have subscribed to the game of success as a means to survive. We need to be honest in our self-assessment in order to illuminate opportunities to remove negative attachments and to better understand ourselves as innovative leaders.

We will question the very notion of work. We will challenge the underpinnings of our educational system in ways that call into question the value we've placed on certifications, degrees, and titles. We are calling for a new perspective on leadership that challenges the old colonial way. Keep in mind that in challenging the old way, we are not attempting to pull your self-worth out from beneath you. We know how disorienting it can be to untether yourself from relevance of the corporate model of success. We honor who you are and recognize how scary it may feel, but we assure you the journey is worth the effort.

As you continue to read, you'll become more aware of the false values that have fueled your sense of self-worth and how they have been holding you back. Perhaps you think that you could *be* more if only you could find the time to *do* more. The corporate mindset may make you feel that being yourself will never be enough. We meet you here at the crossroads of critical voices in your mind. This is where the journey into joy begins, with a massive paradigm shift that will guide you from the outside world and invite you back inside to your heart. Here is where you can create the space to center who you are in self-love and leave behind the struggles, criticisms, and deficits of the past.

We are treading a new path to more humane values that may feel threatening in some ways, but we promise it won't take your breath away. In fact, on this journey, you will finally regain your breath and the stamina that's been depleted by the lonely struggle in your workplace and in your brain. We'll be giving a lot of attention to breath, so as you read, take note of when you hold your breath and when you exhale. Falling in and out of breath are clues to understanding when you are in your heart versus your brain. Our beating hearts and blood need to be oxygenated, so breathe and relax into your breath.

Life is full of wonderment and delight. However, we cannot realize the inherent beauty of life if we keep choosing to operate in ways that do not honor joy, self-love, and the freedom to catch our breath. These are the mechanisms that allow us to more fully realize all the wonderment and delight we seek.

THE MONDAY BLUES

For a multitude of reasons, some people in leadership positions choose to abuse their power. The rules governing our workplaces have been carefully constructed for mastery over people and processes. In the colonial mindset, leaders don't know how to value their teams or even themselves outside the traditional power structure. Control and exploitation is the name of the game.

The expectation that our jobs will drain, exhaust, and deplete us has become so ingrained that our very sense of time operates on these cadences. We start our workweek with "a case of the Mondays" or "the Monday blues." We manage to get to midweek, "hump day," and finally, "TGIF," giving gratitude to a higher power for the simple passing of time and the respite of a two-day weekend (that is, of course, if we're lucky enough to have just one job and a full weekend of rest). All of this is baked into our implicit understanding that work will drain us of something vital at the core of our being. We feel like prisoners of the workweek with occasional time off for good behavior.

One of the first concepts we tackle with our coaching clients at The Big Joy Theory is to simply ask a few questions: What if all this were not a given? What if we didn't dissociate our real lives from our work lives? What if we were not told to leave our hearts at home and only bring our brains to work? What if the tasks that we spend such huge chunks of our time doing were instead energizing, affirming, and joyful? This would require a radical reinterpretation of not only what it means to work but also why and how we in the West—and increasingly, across the globe—have made work into the exhausting chore it currently is. To do that, we must first revisit the histories of work, management, and leadership to understand how they came to be as they are today.

But before we do, let's remind ourselves that rules are only helpful to the extent that they allow people to breathe and become who they were meant to be. By "breathe" we mean freedom, which is almost paradoxical to our current understanding of rules. However, good rules are less like constraints and more like guardrails. Rules of the road, for instance, are not meant to constrain you but to free you to drive safely and reach your destination quickly. Yet, when we look at the rules of work, management, and leadership, we see that those rules are not nearly as freeing and are, in fact, quite constraining.

Most people are actually moving at a slower rate, and in some cases extremely slower, than what they are capable of.

For some people—those who have always had a deep understanding that we were never meant to live by exploitative rules—there is freedom in the recognition that these rules are failing us. For others, to consider that these rules fail us is scary, even terrifying, because so many have become so attached to the rules that society has impressed upon our minds. This is why we must understand their origins, so we can determine whether these rules continue to make sense to us and should stay in our lives, or whether we would like to revisit and rewrite these rules altogether, if even just for ourselves.

ROOTED IN SLAVERY

So many of these rules are deeply linked to Old World capitalist practices that now seem inseparable from "doing business." It can be, and frankly should be, quite jarring to learn where these practices came from.

In the article "How Slavery Inspired Modern Business Management," UC Berkeley professor and historian Caitlin C. Rosenthal recounts a 1911 congressional meeting "to investigate the impact of new business practices on the lives of workers," with a particular interest in scientific management, most commonly associated with Frederick Winslow Taylor, the father of "Taylorism." Taylor, among others, was called to testify, and advocates of scientific management pointed to slavery as a fundamental point of reference for the practice which applies "precise metrics to even basic processes."[1]

Not only does scientific management constantly monitor and evaluate its workers, but it also establishes the role of the manager, from whose perspective "control was the essential characteristic," according to Rosenthal. "Of course, the ticking of a stopwatch is wildly different from the lash of the whip—or a whip and a watch used in tandem, as was the case on some plantations," she continues. "But there is nonetheless something revealing and deeply troubling about the analogy, particularly because proponents of scientific management sometimes used the language of slavery as well—and not to condemn the system but to praise it."[2]

We have seen the language of these management practices adapt and evolve over the years, even to the extent of encompassing its opposite, espousing empowerment and the holistic self. Indeed, corporate speak and scientific management's ability to "code switch," or alter its language for its times and circumstances, is a main reason that it is so easy to remain unaware of its roots. Although thinkers such as Machiavelli and Sun Tzu have long presented what we might call organizational philosophies, most of scientific management has come directly from the church, the military, and the plantation.

---

[1] Rosenthal, Caitlin C. "How Slavery Inspired Modern Business Management." *Boston Review*, 17 Aug. 2018, bostonreview.net/articles/caitlin-c-rosenthal-accounting -slavery-excerpt.

[2] Ibid.

As Columbia University management professor Rita Gunther McGrath shares in her seminal *Harvard Business Review* essay "Management's Three Eras: A Brief History," by the early 1900s, "the term 'management' was in wide use," with theories that "emphasized efficiency, lack of variation, consistency of production and predictability. The goal was to optimize the outputs that could be generated from a specific set of inputs."[3]

With the 1881 founding of the Wharton School at the University of Pennsylvania, the idea of a type of "business leadership" that extended into public life more broadly, as well as the belief that "management was a discipline of growing evidence and evolving theory," became more widespread.[4]

The mid-twentieth century and its so-called "guru-industrial complex" ushered in a form of management that emphasized expertise. Insights from other fields such as sociology and psychology were brought in, and "statistical and mathematical insights were imported (often from military uses) forming the basis of what would subsequently be known as operations management. Later attempts to bring science into management included the development of the theory of constraints, management by objectives, reengineering," and so on.[5]

---

[3] McGrath, Rita Gunther. "Management's Three Eras: A Brief History." *Harvard Business Review*, 2 Nov. 2014, hbr.org/2014/07/managements-three-eras-a-brief-history.

[4] Ibid.

[5] Ibid.

No matter how much management theories evolve, however, they cannot be divorced from their roots. Princeton sociologist Matthew Desmond shares the following in a famous *New York Times Magazine* article:

The surprising bit has to do with the many eerily specific ways slavery can still be felt in our economic life. "American slavery is necessarily imprinted on the DNA of American capitalism," write the historians Sven Beckert and Seth Rockman. The task now, they argue, is "cataloging the dominant and recessive traits" that have been passed down to us, tracing the unsettling and often unrecognized lines of descent by which America's national sin is now being visited upon the third and fourth generations.[6]

Following Rosenthal's line of thinking, Desmond continues:

Perhaps you're reading this at work, maybe at a multinational corporation that runs like a soft-purring engine. You report to someone, and someone reports to you. Everything is tracked, recorded, and analyzed, via vertical reporting systems, double-entry record-keeping, and precise quantification. Data seems to hold sway over every operation. It

---

[6] Desmond, Matthew. "In Order to Understand the Brutality of American Capitalism, You Have to Start on the Plantation." *New York Times Magazine*, 14 Aug. 2019, nytimes.com/interactive/2019/08/14/magazine/slavery-capitalism.html.

feels like a cutting-edge approach to management, but many of these techniques that we now take for granted were developed by and for large plantations.[7]

And that's just considering the data-driven management and decision-making approaches that are so popular now. Where do you think interviewing, annual reviews, promotions, terminations, and almost any other leadership or management practice come from? Almost universally, they come from the military, the church, and/ or the plantation. This, of course, does not make them inherently bad. But if you have never envisioned yourself within the confines of work in those domains, it may surprise you to learn that you've been operating within them all along.

The key takeaway is simply that individuals and communities with freedom were never meant to be organized in the ways that we now find ourselves. We were always supposed to be free and feel our humanity ushered forward in a way that is helpful, supportive, and even empowering.

---

[7] Desmond, 2019.

The Game of the Corporate Mindset

We are often taught to play the game of the corporate mindset in order to obtain a sense of security in a job that will pay for the life we hope to have one day. So many leaders must also overcome the historical burdens of genocide, slavery, systematic disempowerment (as in the case of gender), and/or complete dehumanization (as in the case of differences in physical ability). It therefore becomes reasonable for our brains, in the name of survival, to subscribe to the notion that safety exists in playing by the rules of a system that is outside of us, one that has already turned against us and countless others. In our hearts, we may know that such endeavors are of the riskiest kind, but our brains convince us that we have no choice.

NURTURE YOUR SENSE OF SELF

Just as a gardener tends to her plantings, real leadership is about nurturing what may flourish within you, given the right amount of light, energy, guidance, and love. This is the way the world was supposed to work, and we just have to look to nature to prove it. The gardener supports her new seedlings with stakes to guide their growth. Even trees are often secured with stakes for the first year or two to ensure they grow upright. This is how models of leadership can, and should, operate. They can guide us along a path of growth and development that helps us become productive members of and contributors to healthy communities, much as a tree grows strong in a tended orchard.

It is important that core pillars of the corporate mindset model, namely the mechanisms and frameworks of leadership, evolve beyond the inherited hierarchies and instead center all people and their individual expressions of who they are as leaders. This, fundamentally, is the failure of most of today's leadership. We continue to subscribe to models of leadership that were birthed in the Industrial Revolution, models that came from the military, the plantation, or the church, all of which are inherently hierarchical and oriented around a standard of basic survival. This is not conducive to the modern workplace where survival shouldn't be the baseline—rather, creativity, growth, and innovation should be. We can't simply tweak the old models and apply them to such a drastically different paradigm and aspiration. We must remove the old models altogether and replace them with new ones that promote empowerment over management, freedom over fear, joy over jealousy.

A leadership model that centers the love, light, and wisdom of each leader will cultivate more space for each person to bring their true gifts to the world. However, the current practice of leadership smothers the gifts within each soul, blocking the light that so many people need to grow. Ask yourself, at what age were you told that you couldn't do what you loved to make money in this world? When were you told that you had to just follow orders? We know to give a plant the appropriate amount of light, but we forget to do the same for our own growth, ignoring our hearts.

We buy plants for our offices because they provide joy, yet we don't have the same mindset to nurture ourselves as leaders. Corporate America naively does the opposite with its mechanisms of control. It's time for organizations to nurture the human heart in the workplace.

Just as forests need biodiversity to flourish, organizations need diverse, creative, and innovative solutions for the workplace to flourish. There is so much opportunity for humanity to grow beyond the hierarchical one-size-fits-all models of leadership. When people are nurtured in the workplace, the community of leaders in each organization can flourish. The organization itself will flourish and innovate for a better world.

> Joy is the highest vibration of your own inner light that illuminates your true path to leadership.

And the most effective way to do this is through joy. It is only through the lens of joy that we can empower ourselves to work effectively and optimally. We need a joy mindset to replace the corporate mindset. Leading-edge thinkers, theorists, and entrepreneurs are aware of the need for this positive disruption in how we "organize" the workplace. The solution is right under our noses—specifically, in our hearts—just waiting to be uncovered and brought to bear to facilitate our individual and collective evolution. Joy is the highest vibration of your own inner light that illuminates your own true path to leadership.

Moreover, time is of the essence for this world to realize that the leadership structure in corporate America is holding people back. We know that the gaps in society are everywhere and growing. There are wealth gaps, ethnicity gaps, gender gaps, pay gaps, equality gaps, and more popping up and ballooning. This is why we must reexamine the very foundational principles of our leadership model.

Few entrusted with leadership have proven to know the wisdom of their own hearts. The ethics of leadership have been unmonitored for too long and are consequently unraveling across every industry and sector. The world is ready to advance, and our framework for leadership needs to advance with it. Yet rather than tearing down the old structures, we can just let them go, and instead lead from a place of self-love.

We realize this is a challenging concept that may inspire fear, uncertainty, or doubt in some of you. But know that your own self-love can serve as the guardrails along your journey of leadership. You don't have to fear failure or not meeting someone else's expectations. As Mahatma Gandhi is often quoted, "Be the change you wish to see in the world."

Each person, each leader, has an internal mechanism to hone their own sense of self-love in a way that holds them accountable. When this happens, people grow from their mistakes, learn from their own growth, listen to best practices, co-create, and innovate new mechanisms of growth and development. This is the path forward that ensures everyone gets the light they need to grow in a way that is meaningful to them. This is the path to a world that can evolve past fear and control to truth and success.

Chapter 2

UNSPOKEN RULES OF THE CORPORATE MINDSET

The corporate mindset and its status quo thinking are keeping humanity from advancing, halting progress in its tracks. The multitude of ways in which people feel stifled in their own growth is causing unprecedented levels of anxiety, depression, stress, chronic pain, and immune disorders. People fear they aren't strong enough to make it in this world without the tired old rules. As one of our clients described it: leaders in the workplace will rise only until they find their breaking point, where they will get crushed under the weight of it all.

We experience the corporate mindset when we feel it brush up against our humanity. Sometimes it's subtle, and sometimes it's as blatant as a stinking onion that brings tears to our eyes. We choke down those tears, which become a heavy burden. We are left overwhelmed, not knowing what to do. Avoiding the issue only gives the corporate mindset more power. Some rebel and become ensnared in the fight, responding and reacting in opposition.

The corporate mindset leads to "yes men" who strive for the corner office. It is the root of employee disengagement and why meaningful work is so often absent from the workplace. It simply cannot honor or acknowledge the work that really matters. It is this mindset that seeps beyond the business world into all aspects of our lives, including our media, and underpins how the accumulation of expensive possessions is the only universally accepted and valid indicator of success.

A leader could present with clinical mental illness, unethical behavior, and slovenly professional practices and still be touted as a good leader, provided they are wealthy and have the right title, degrees, and pedigree. A prime example of all this is academic grade point average (GPA). A person's GPA is, in fact, not correlated to success in life. This has been proven over and over again at every level of education.

Yet each new generation of parents pushes their children to be at the top of the class, to have the highest grades they can possibly achieve, so as to get to the next rung, which is really more about the fear of not "getting ahead." Parents want to know that their child will be okay after they are gone. However, many parents don't realize how distanced they have become from their own humanity in their own work lives. This is the same mindset that led to the 2020 college admissions scandal, where cheating in the name of academic advancement was somehow justified by otherwise honest people.

In this environment, where is the care and concern for our next generation of leaders? How can we ensure that they effectively develop healthy models of self-love? Where is the model of what real success looks like without having to "fake it until you make it?"

So pervasive is this thinking that even those who are waking up to the game still often tout half-true rules of thumb: "Get a degree, get a job, get money, and you'll be successful." "Work hard; play hard." Buying into false truths in the name of staying within social norms comes at the expense of freedom and innovation. Every person deserves a meaningful education, yes. College does expand one's skills and network. But academic success alone is an insufficient measure of a leader's real value, let alone a life well lived.

> The corporate mindset is the seemingly endless list of unspoken rules of the workplace environment.

The corporate mindset has done such a phenomenal job of inundating us with so many superficial measures of success that even when we achieve real joy and success in our lives, we doubt ourselves and question if it is real. Most often we assume it was a fluke or good luck. Even those already in top leadership positions regularly question if some of their best accomplishments make them worthy. The danger is that people's highest and most authentic expression of self has been so diminished that when leaders experience their own joy, they don't know how to relish it. They don't recognize their own heart in action. Looking in the mirror, they question who they see.

The corporate mindset is the seemingly endless list of unspoken rules of the workplace environment, rules that reinforce the illusion of a linear path to success and validate the hierarchy of power that, in turn, sets the tone, energy, and business practices that drive organizations, and thereby the rules of our "modern" society.

THE RULES

The corporate mindset has its own rules. Here are just a few:

- Leadership is top-down.
- There is little room at the top for leaders.
- Good employees fit into the culture of the organization.
- Employees are to toe the company line.
- Fear and stress are good motivators for performance.
- Work comes first. Personal stuff stays at home.
- Conflict is a problem.
- Diversity is a burden.

Do any of these rules take your breath away? Do they ring true to your own experience? Now, take a breath and notice that there is so little room for self-love in these rules that leaders only have space to move from fear and control. There is no air to breathe for those who follow these rules, nor is there any wisdom to be gained.

Let's take a moment here to clarify that when we speak of breath, we are not simply speaking of the act of exhaling and inhaling but of the very energy it produces. It's the sensation we each get when we just stop for a moment, focus on our breath, and feel the cool touch of new fresh air enter our bodies. Then we feel the warm gliding of our exhalation as it exits our nostrils. It is the sensation of space, freedom, and peace.

We distill this down to the word "breath" and invite you, upon reading the word, to revisit it and take a meaningful and peaceful breath as you continue to read. In doing so, you begin to unlock the grip of the mistruths of the corporate mindset you've been pressured to assume, all the way down to the relevance of how quickly you read and finish this book. By getting back in touch with yourself, you will begin to open the requisite space to live your own sense of self and become a person who leads with joy.

Finding breath will also allow you to more clearly see that the old colonial mindset is a system of unspoken rules built on lies and illusions sustained by fear. In fact, subscribing to these rules walks a leader out of their own heart and soul. The rules of the corporate mindset mandate that everything on the outside comes before your own internal humanity. You are held accountable for fitting in until you are fragmented and unable to breathe. Finally, you must somehow find a way to perform, get to the top, and fight to stay there, all while feeling disconnected from yourself.

OUT OF BREATH, BACKWARD, AND UPSIDE-DOWN

Leading without breathing has been so normalized that it is expected. All the innate qualities we possess to become great leaders are, at best, nice-to-have "soft skills," but not essential. Only the "hard skills" matter in the corporate mindset, while we ignore and devalue the very skills we need to empower one another, to connect, and to reflect another's humanity. In fact, the corporate mindset has fully weaponized self-love.

In the corporate mindset, self-love is conflated with ego, such that leaders often avoid operating out of self-love for fear that they might love themselves too much and become egomaniacal or narcissistic. Yet true self-love is not egoistic. Egomaniacs and narcissists don't actually love themselves. They are lacking in self-love, so much so that they have stopped valuing the wisdom of their own hearts completely. This is why they need so much validation from the outside world. It is why they default to thinking that they are better than others or deserving of more attention than their peers for superficial reasons. It is also why, interestingly, they tend to do rather well within the corporate mindset—their relentless pursuit of external validation plays well in a model that claims the only meaningful validation comes from outside of you. They need to believe this, or they feel they are worth nothing.

In reality, the egoic frame of mind is the outcome not of genuine self-love but the love of power. In the colonial mindset, leaders who operate out of ego are more valued. The world sees them as tough and efficient, and mistakes self-centeredness for having a center. Self-love requires self-knowledge, which is something that the corporate mindset places no value upon.

Self-love is a deep state of gratitude for oneself that grows from seeing one's truths and values authentically expressed in the world in a way that supports our physical, psychological, and energetic growth. Self-love is at the root of authentic leadership. How can one "walk their own talk" without knowing who they are in their own heart? They can't. This is why we must reintegrate self-love into the heart of leadership. Fear of self-love is inherent in the colonial model of success. Once we remove that fear from the equation, the pathway to being powered by joy and fully expressed in your heart becomes clear.

Self-love does not have to be the quiet, lonely journey that it often is today. Instead, it can be centered in humanity as a critical component of leading well. Love is a better indicator of self-awareness than many of the more formal psychological assessments, such as self-awareness, self-esteem, or well-being. Assessment scales talk about what we like, what we know, and how we do things, but never about the foundation from which we do them.

The Rosenberg Self-Esteem Scale is perhaps as close as we get, but still there is no assessment of the extent to which one loves oneself. The scale rightly measures the extent to which one feels that they are a person of worth, but then qualifies that with "at least on an equal plane with others." Inherent in the measure is a suggestion that we can only understand our own sense of worth in comparison to others and not what we intuitively know or feel we can do. The assessment also asks whether the responder "agrees" or "disagrees" with whether they "feel that they are able to do things as well as most other people." [8]

This is the inherent flaw, not in the assessments, per se, but in the very approach we take in trying to understand ourselves. It was never meant to be an externally measured scale. It matters far less how you feel you compare to someone else, and far more that you feel you are becoming a better version of you. But this requires that we let go of egoic competition and replace it with self-love that inspires co-creation.

Logic that rejects the corporate mindset suggests that individuals with self-love are more likely to have an accurate assessment of who they are in the world than those who do not. This is true simply for the minimization of all the cognitive distortions that come with thinking that competition comes out of ego and that our worth and understanding of ourselves is based on external comparisons to others: family, friends, colleagues, strangers, billionaires, and so on. Self-love is a cleaner, clearer, and more accurate measure

---

[8] Rosenberg, M. (1965). *Rosenberg Self-Esteem Scale* (RSES) [Database record]. APA PsycTests.

that someone is developing in their authentic leadership. There are over seven billion people out there; are you really going to compare yourself to all of them?

It is very important to name these effects of the corporate mindset because at some point between the first day of school and today, you've almost certainly noticed that something is terribly wrong with a system that promotes so many deficient, dysfunctional leaders—and even abusive ones—to the top. Having a model of leadership that turns leaders backward and flips them upside-down in their own evolution is an intolerable misfortune that our hearts simply cannot suffer anymore.

For many, the old mindset seemed unfair, but tolerable enough, until the leader running the company or country started resembling a villain in a horror movie. There is no true self-love in such a leader—one can hardly see them breathing. Such leaders make decisions from a bottom-line profit model they learned in business school. They run entire organizations, entire countries, and cover up their own insecurities and unresolved traumas, blatantly operating out of ego. This is when it all turns upside-down because what one thought was the pinnacle of success, be it the C-suite or Oval Office, is merely a pretension to happiness. Meanwhile, the average worker is left to internalize the colonial mindset and all its rules, and learn to normalize an antiquated model of leadership that puts profits before people.

STEEPED IN TRAUMA

Backward and upside-down, many leaders become so stressed that they succumb to abusive leadership behaviors in the name of survival. Most of these behaviors, like using fear, control, and manipulation, have been so normalized that to call attention to them is considered insubordination. To get along, one must simply put up with it. If you can't handle it, then you are weak, right? Yet there is another layer of abusive leadership behavior with such a level of intensity that most are not able to put up with it on their best days. That layer is actually mental illness and undiagnosed personality disorders that have been masquerading as drive and high motivation.

Mental illness is running rampant in our homes, communities, and workspaces. We can see it most clearly in children whose mal-adjustments are typically handled with psychoactive medications. As these kids get older, little is resolved, because taking medications does not diminish the root trauma. At best, it reduces symptoms, but the origins of trauma are rarely addressed. Our education experts are not equipped for it, nor is the medical establishment sufficiently encouraged to provide the right kind of treatment. Consequently, those kids become adults with the same untreated traumas still dogging their lives. Eventually, they enter a workspace ill-equipped to deal with mental health issues.

The corporate mindset simply does not value the mental health of its workforce, nor of its leaders. Even increased access to mental health services and stress reduction initiatives fail to address the degree of mental health concerns showing up at work.

We tolerate the bad behavior of leaders as long as they continue to perform and maintain positive outcomes. Meanwhile, the negative effects accumulate, wreaking havoc on the mental health and well-being of their teams. Far too many staff members and leaders report being triggered by their boss's bad behavior. Over 85 percent of the coaching we do is focused on helping leaders to safely navigate their bosses' unresolved traumas that cause them to feel insecure and threatened or to act out of character for self-preservation. And because most people have some sort of unresolved trauma from their childhoods, a boss's inability to cope with their mental state can send colleagues and teams further into their brains for cover.

Your degree and job experience can put you on a trajectory of success, but even then, you may wind up working for the wrong leader with unresolved trauma. Your work life can slip into an alternate universe where your entire mission in life is to keep your boss happy. Your very identity, be it your race, gender, age, LGBTQIA+ identity, nationality, native language, or ability level, can all be interpreted as threats by your traumatized boss. Your degrees become insufficient. Your years of experience, irrelevant. If you have not yet mastered a particular skill, your social capital may be significantly diminished. Make a small error and all hell might break loose. Like in the game of chutes and ladders, back under someone's thumb/ego you go.

Trying to succeed under the burden of someone else's fragile ego will trigger just about anyone's trauma. We've found that leaders who had already started to bring heart and self-love into their work were still tanked by their own trauma when faced with tyrannical bosses. They were shocked to be confronting the very same feelings they thought they had overcome years ago when they moved out of their parents' home.

In the world of the colonial mindset, the cycle of trauma goes round and round. Too many leaders hold unresolved trauma from dysfunctional families that gets triggered by the very model of success they are trying to conform to. The traumas of our leaders have not been adequately addressed throughout their lives. Not by their families. Not by the educational system. Instead, they have been further triggered by stress at work. So, by the time you came along, the only move left was to burden you with their troubles. If you are willing to take one for the team, perhaps you still get to climb that ladder. But choose the sanity of your own heart, and you are not a team player.

This dynamic undermines the innate human desire to be whole and heart-centered. Amazing and passionate leaders show up in a workspace with high hopes that are so often dashed against walls of conflict born of trauma.

WHAT TRAUMA SOUNDS LIKE

As coaches, we've truly heard it all. Below are near verbatim quotes from clients in their first or second session with us, while still steeped in corporate-mindset thinking. We invite you to read each one and see if you can determine where the leader got stuck in the game of success.

Here's what trauma sounds like from the mouths and souls of leaders stuck in the corporate mindset:

- "I don't know if I am good enough."
- "If you don't need me, how will you ever like me?"
- "I did everything everyone asked me to do. I was the good little boy/girl. Why isn't everything working out?"
- "Yes, I am good at math/art/strategy/tactics/relationship building/technology/sales/marketing." (The list goes on, but these are actual examples we've heard from clients.) "But how am I ever going to be a good leader?"
- "I thought that my struggle was the cost to live in this country."
- "I really want this job. But I'm not sure they'll ever respect someone like me."
- "I'm just going to stick it out for a little while, like three to five years, seven, or maybe ten, max ten, and then I can start my [passion] business."

- "I thought that I was going to have to save everyone for free just so I could be unburdened enough to lead, one day."
- "It somehow became relevant for me to take responsibility for the losses, to preserve my relationship with the people that I love."
- "If I am not fighting, then how can I still be a Black woman?"

Can you discern where each leader got stuck? That moment in their lives where one of the rules of the corporate mindset wedged itself in, and made itself relevant, if not fundamental, to their model of success? At the beginning of their work with us, each of these leaders was stuck in a deficit-oriented mindset with little space to breathe or love themselves, let alone to see and embrace the leader they were becoming. You can hear it loudly in each of the phrases above. But just to make sure, let's take a moment to fully clarify how to identify the corporate mindset when it presents itself in your life.

KNOW THE CORPORATE MINDSET WHEN YOU SEE IT

In a recent article, Tony Schwartz, the CEO of The Energy Project, which is a leading team in the organizational improvement industry, and Christine Porath, a tenured professor at Georgetown University's McDonough School of Business, shined some much-needed light on a collective dirty secret: most of us hate our jobs.[9] They noted several key statistics of what we lack in the workplace.

Key Factors Lacking in the Workplace

- Regular time for creative or strategic thinking (70 percent lack this at work)
- Ability to focus on one thing at a time (66 percent lack this at work)
- Opportunities to do most enjoyed tasks (60 percent lack this at work)
- Level of meaning and significance (50 percent lack this at work)
- Connection to company's mission (50 percent lack this at work)
- A sense of community (49 percent lack this at work)

Their list goes on, but we would also like to add that most workplaces also do not allow for the following:

- Strengths-based ways of thinking and being
- Honest, joyful experiences and celebrations of success in life
- A model of leadership that advances you into being the leader you want to be

---

[9] Schwartz, Tony and Porath, Christine. "Why You Hate Work." *New York Times*, 1 Jun 2014, nytimes.com/2014/06/01/opinion/sunday/why-you-hate-work.html.

The good news is that the problem is not with you. It is just the way our systems and processes continue to diminish the relevance of our hearts, our wisdom, and joy in our work. The colonial mindset doesn't want that "nonsense" for itself, or for you either. So, let's stop masquerading. Here's a quick checklist to see if you're already head-deep in the masquerade at the corporate ball.

Checklist for Masquerading at the Corporate Ball

Have a go at this list—check off any that apply to you:

- ☐ You wince at the thought of going into work each morning. But you still put on the clothes (and makeup), do your hair, and get out there and do it, in spite of yourself.
- ☐ You somehow find yourself sitting at your desk each morning, coffee in hand, not really remembering how you got there, let alone why you're really there.
- ☐ Your state of fuck-it-ness with the humdrum of status quo leadership is increasing as indicated by the number of times that you say "man, fuck this shit" or sigh while at work.
- ☐ You have already disengaged from various meetings before you even show up because you know that nothing is going to get accomplished...again.
- ☐ You are at work but not in the work; you know that you don't like your job or even the people you work

with, and your primary motivation for being there is the benefits.

☐ You have a side hustle that no one at work knows about. You sneak time and energy at work thinking about and planning how you are going to do more of that because it is what really makes you happy.

☐ There is a big difference between "weekend you" and "workday you" because you have bottled up all your freaky goodness and shoved it into a suit Monday through Friday.

☐ You are exhausted at the end of the day from putting on a facade for the past eight to nine hours.

☐ You are operating from your brain, thinking, worrying, and ruminating about pretty much everything, and not consistently in your heart.

We know that when we can clearly identify the features listed above, either within the organization (as detailed by The Energy Project's list) or within ourselves (as described in our checklist for Masquerading at the Corporate Ball), we then begin to recognize that what we're really seeing is the corporate mindset in action.

To be clear, the idea here is not to create some sort of binary or diagnosis protocol. Instead, these are the symptoms, and with enough symptoms, you can begin to isolate and identify the disease. One or two of these showing up some of the time probably does not warrant you jumping up in the middle of a board meeting, pointing your finger, and yelling, "J'accuse! Corporate mindset thinking!" But certainly, the more boxes you tick, the greater the likelihood is that what you are experiencing is the corporate mindset at work in your life.

TO THINE OWN HEART BE TRUE

Leaders are silently suffering in the bowels of corporate America. This is something that we must stop avoiding and get comfortable acknowledging, because people—good, well-intentioned leaders— are waiting for someone to hear them. Until we do, they sit in their own suffering waiting to be released from the pain, often darkness, all around them. And because they are not whole and breathing, they are causing each other very real harm. You will understand this better as we continue, but for now, know that this is what we mean when we say that the weeds take over.

These leaders, triggered into their own unresolved trauma, are no longer flowers. They are operating like weeds: trying to take over, claim power, and manage other people and anything they can get their hands on, all to ensure their own safety. This is the real weight of the colonial mindset that is crushing people and making it difficult for people to grow, let alone flourish.

Much of the fighting in this world has nothing to do with the real work to be done. It is a distraction. It is not that the people are unimportant, or their causes not worth fighting for. There was simply never supposed to be all this fighting in the first place. Because of all the struggle in the world, people think that leading well is to fight well, when fighting at all is just distraction. Right now, most people—at least far too many leaders—are turned backward and upside-down in their own sense of who they are, fighting to be relevant in their boss's mind when their value in this world should have been granted to them the minute they took their first breath. Therefore, it is time to let the corporate mindset go, and time to get back to our hearts.

Self-love is the key to recenter joy in your world and shift out of the constant struggle: The struggle to be good. The struggle to do good. The struggle to be valued by others for the goodness in your heart. The struggle against every layer of oppression.

But when the rules of the corporate mindset say that the only relevance in this world is your title, your salary, and your performance at work as evaluated by your manager, then it is really no wonder at all that leaders become so lost in their own evolution. The real challenge is that the rules designed to acknowledge trauma and harm at work are left to be managed by an under-resourced, ineffectual, and largely powerless person who is simply plodding along in the human resources department. We even acknowledge this with cruel phrases like "winners don't work in HR" (an actual quote overheard multiple times while attending an "elite" business school).

Life brings about change. This is inherent to the beauty of life. When things are living, they need space to evolve. Most people look at evolution as a thing of the past. It is not. It is literally happening right now. It is happening to you. It is happening to the tree outside your window. It is happening to the planet and to the universe. Humans have not evolved to their highest level; they're still evolving. This is important to name as it calls forward the opportunity for all people to grow, to keep growing, and to be grateful and excited for the journey. We cannot grow, will not see the need to grow, or will miss hearing the invitation to grow if we think that evolution is something that has already happened in the past, something to be studied and not lived. Evolution must be lived in every breath, every decision, each and every opportunity. That is true living.

Living requires the freedom to breathe, and so we need to create and cultivate rules in organizations that allow people to breathe so that leaders can breathe, so that organizations can breathe. Organizations that do not breathe become constrained and, sooner or later, seize up and cease to exist. Trying to hold on to "the market" is exactly what kills so many organizations, some faster than others. The decision to not breathe or grow leads to the eventual downfall of a company as it would any living organism. An organization breathes when all its people can breathe and therefore grow, individually and collectively. It is less about finding ways to keep people embedded in the fabric of the culture, and more about letting them bring the fabric of their culture to the organization so that the biodiversity the community needs to grow can manifest.

It is time for organizations to create space to heal their community of leaders, from the inside out. The journey to healing, and its necessary discomforts, must stop being weaponized as a problem. It is not a problem that people are trying to breathe beyond their traumas. The problem is that without models of leadership that allow for this work, there is insufficient support for leaders to do their own work correctly.

> Leading without joy is simply distraction.

Properly healing from trauma—not just trying to apply a band-aid—effectively brings leaders back into their own self-love, which is exactly where they will find their breath, talents, strengths, wisdom, and joy. And in the end, they will perform better, they will lead better, and they will contribute more value to themselves, to those around them, and to the world.

Organizations keep looking in the wrong direction to improve productivity and decrease costs, and it is literally costing them everything, including the very money and time they are so desperate to save. Imagine if your organization could just take a year to help all its people to heal and regain their own sense of self-worth. What would it mean for the future of your organization, and for all the leaders, families, and communities it touches?

Leading without joy is simply distraction. This is why it is so vital that we shift the rules of the corporate mindset away from external mechanisms of fear and control and toward the internal power of joy.

Chapter 3

LEADING OUTSIDE
THE BOX

The corporate mindset boxes each of us into a rigid framework. In this mindset, we each exist within our own confined physical space and place in linear time. The walls of the box are adorned with our accomplishments as we each struggle on our own to acquire an even bigger box with more accomplishments, more tools, more knowledge, more possessions. And we each struggle desperately for more time to accomplish all the tasks contained within our solitary box.

Inside the box, time is measured in years, days, and hours in perpetual linear sequence, ticking away every fleeting minute and second, one after another. How many minutes have you spent wondering how many minutes you have left? This notion of time keeps humanity boxed in. And time is used to distract and control the ways in which humans measure success. This is where the concept of measuring success by how much we do in a day comes from. It is why so many people are focused on checking off to-do lists.

We were taught this notion of time when we were small children playing with blocks and dollhouses. We'd build our imaginary homes, castles, and cities. We'd pretend a box was a car, a bus, or a spaceship, and in that moment, boxes were our entire world. As time went on and we attended school in big, boxy brick buildings, we learned to advance from one educational box to the next, passing grades and earning degrees and certificates. This became the measure of our lives and our time, moving along in linear fashion, from one year to the next. Yet, despite our progression from smaller to larger boxes—be it the small elementary school to the larger high school to the yet larger university, or from the starter home with tiny rooms to bigger houses with open layouts—we still, in the end, find ourselves completely boxed in.

> We can finally stop feeling that we must suffer alone.

In order to expand outside the rigid confines of living boxed in, we need to understand that time is cyclical rather than linear. Although we age year by year, our time is marked by cyclical phases: the changing of seasons, the daily rising and setting of the sun, the ever-cyclical phases of the moon. Just as the patterns of planets and stars move in cycles and orbits, so do our lives. We come into being and live out our days as distinct people, but when we pass on, the atoms we are comprised of return to the universe. Our souls, our consciousness, and the energy that was once us disperses back to its source. This is the cycle of life and time.

In the same way, we need a new understanding of success in life and work that isn't contained in a series of boxes following a linear progression. Within the confinement of a box, whether small or large, access to air is limited. Everything is then judged by the linear passing of time spent in a given box. You took more than a year to pass a grade, more than four years to finish high school or college. You stayed in a job or relationship too long, or perhaps not long enough. All of these presume that the box is real, that the time measured in that box is relevant, and that there is an order and a speed to life. There isn't, and operating as if there is, is exactly what steals our breath.

Rather than living in linear fashion from beginning to end, we can forever expand and open up the broad middle, that which is constantly unfolding with every breath, every decision, every experience. Stepping outside the box, we can see further with a yet wider vision of what's possible. We enter a cyclical flow where energy is shared in community and expanded in self. We begin to stop seeing other people as threats and begin seeing them as partners on a shared journey. We improve the way we relate to ourselves and the people around us.

There was never a need for the confinement of a box, but there is a need for relationship, including relationship to ourselves with self-love, which empowers us. Choosing to love ourselves opens us to the wisdom of joy inherent in each of us. Outside the breathless box, we "come into our own" and discover we have everything we need to reach our potential for success.

When we can each breathe freely, nothing is limited or constrained. We can stop fighting for air and feel breath as an infinite resource. We open to each other and trust our hearts. Our decisions evolve from love, caring, and mutual concern for one another. We can finally stop feeling that we must suffer alone. We come to understand that we are one people, one universe, with common goals. More than a mindset, this is the new *heartset* we need in troubling times.

COMING INTO SELF-LOVE

When we break free of our solitary boxes, we understand what it means to be one with ourselves and others. We no longer have to fight desperately for our share. This has been the evolving story of our lives, perhaps best exemplified in the experience of Jax's evolution. Jax was socialized in the same corporate mindset we all were. Small in physical stature, she strove to become the shortest Division I high jumper in the country, overcoming every obstacle along the way, and even achieving some of the highest accolades within her sport. Her evolution was a process of learning to follow her own sense of love over constant competition and struggle.

Most leaders think that their leadership journey started later in life than it actually did. Jax thought so too, but she came to understand that leadership starts when we start to lead ourselves. She was raised in a family that was unsafe to love. Many times, she was asked to put her sense of self-love aside so that someone else's struggle could take center stage. At the time, it seemed like the only way to handle her family's life situation.

As the first African Americans to move into an all-white, upper-middle-class neighborhood in 1969, Jax's parents had come to focus on overcoming struggle, putting out fires, and conquering obstacles in their daily lives. It seemed necessary and pertinent to do so. In a world tanked by deficits, fighting for a foothold seemed like the only way, the only hope for Jax's family to find a way to make it.

So when her parents were fighting, or her brother was having trouble in school, or her cousins were desperate for help, Jax was asked to hold her breath. Her needs were constantly put on hold in the name of saving family members in more desperate straits. Jax had to learn to be a pretty good fighter on her own—a warrior, in fact. But self-love was put aside. It seemed to have no value.

So Jax worked overtime to ensure that she could accomplish what she needed and wanted to do before she went off to help others. She did this in silence and out of sight because it didn't feel safe to share her personal triumphs with her family. They would have felt threatened by her choice to put herself first, and they would have weaponized her budding sense of self-love against her in the name of putting family, and all its drama and trauma, first.

For survival, Jax kept her needs to herself and quietly nurtured her own breath and heart. After all, how could she be of service to her family if she couldn't find enough air to breathe? To avoid being labeled selfish and to have energy in reserve to deal with her family's various crises, she had to keep her own struggles and fights to herself.

Does this story sound familiar? The things we are all asked to do in the name of serving and helping others is not unique to Jax. Perhaps you know this story as your story too—perhaps all too well. We are each being asked to live and lead from a place that takes us out of our breath and keeps us disconnected from our own self-love, light, and joy. This is the trap that good leaders fall prey to in the name of "getting ahead" and being a "high performer" within the corporate mindset. And once we have fallen into the trap, it can be very difficult to climb out.

It can take an entire lifetime of struggle to find our way back to self-love. Yet, this competitive approach to living is being passed on from one generation to the next, rooted in our cultures and our family hierarchies. It is causing younger generations to stall without access to self-love. For love of self is required for living. And it is required for leading well.

Jax had to evolve into her own, and on the way, she became a fierce believer in each person's right to love themselves on their journey in life. Less important than becoming a 5' 4" high-jumping champion, Jax's evolution on the battlefields of her life centers on becoming a person who leads with her own authentic leadership presence. She learned to give herself permission to ground herself and embrace her own sense of leadership from her heart.

> We need to lead from the wisdom of our own joy.

It is time to lead with an understanding of who we truly are, regardless of the old corporate mindset and standards. It is critical for leaders to stop performing as leaders in a box devoid of air, organized by a system of exploitation. Leadership can no longer be about aligning with standards of success outside of ourselves. To become effective leaders, we need to evolve to inspire ourselves and others. We need to lead from the wisdom of our own joy with the highest and most authentic expression of our own self-love.

When we let our joy work for us, we can then lead naturally in truly productive and impactful ways. Joy releases us, helps us slow down and step out of judgments and measurements. We engage the world from a place of love and self-empowerment, bringing joy to others as we do so.

FROM FIGHT TO LOVE

The rules of the corporate mindset were not established with self-love in mind. Fear is its primary motivational mechanism, keeping leaders operating in fight-or-flight mode.

In our advisory work, we partner with incredible leaders who are frustrated and tired of having to work against the very organizations that hired them—often, ironically, with the specific directive to lead change and transformation in the workplace. We smile with deep understanding for all their efforts to leverage their strengths and fortitude, for we were once there, trying to do the same, all in the name of good leadership.

This is what a client expressed during one of their first sessions:

The way I see it, at each stage of the game, we are told what we are doing is wrong or not good enough. In first grade, you're not smart enough for second grade, and so on. Even now, as successful as I am, I'm not yet good enough to be a partner in the firm. And so, at each of these stages, you have two choices of how to respond. Either (a), you have the strength and fortitude to see it as a challenge and rise up to meet it, or (b), you get crushed under the weight of all that criticism because either you aren't strong enough or aren't good enough. I think I found the place where option (b) is true for me.

Take a moment to let that sit. Reread it if you have to. See, hear, and feel the sadness. Feel the frustration and helplessness. The shame. Then consider just how true that deficit-oriented model is for so many people, probably including you at some level. We have all lived this model. This is what we were given, and it is time to give it back.

The way we engage with our clients in our work at The Big Joy Theory is to leverage the wisdom of our own joyful evolution to call them back into their heart where their humanity resides. This is far more important, to them, to us, and to the rest of the world, than putting themselves at risk of being crushed by the demands of work. We wholeheartedly, but not so softly, remind them that the rules of the corporate mindset are counterproductive and hypercritical of individuals. For centuries, the colonial mindset has socialized us out of the relevance of our own humanity. We are virtual slaves to the old mindset, but our liberation lies within us, in our hearts.

To assist and watch leaders awaken from the haze of the corporate mindset is always incredible to witness. It is like seeing the lights of a soul slowly flicker back on and resume with full wonderment and delight after being in a trance. To be elevated in self-love and bathed in one's own light is so much more effective a place from which to operate. From this vantage point, one can far more readily see all the traps and triggers in the playing field. We see more clearly how hearts and souls have been sidelined and smothered for lack of breath.

For too long, leaders have been forced to operate without oxygen. It's time to breathe and embrace a new perception of leadership beyond credentials, career, and accolades. It's time to stop fighting the machine and embrace the new model of leadership.

Imagine you're walking down the street and some person you don't know, clearly disheveled and probably psychologically disturbed, begins to yell horrible things at you. They call you every name in the book. What would you do? Do you internalize their toxicity? Do you rationalize with this individual and explain to them how their perceptions of you are incorrect? Do you angrily shout back and tell them that they're crazy and wrong? Or do you do your best to simply ignore them, not allow their negative energy to enter you, and go about your day as best you can, being you? Clearly the best strategy is the last.

Yet most of us are not choosing it. We invite you to consider the criticisms of the corporate mindset as equal to the ravings of a lunatic. Never take criticism from those whom you wouldn't also take advice. Be wary of those who advise or mentor without the wisdom of heart.

The path to leadership unfolds within the heart of each person, sometimes quickly, sometimes slowly, sometimes directly, and sometimes circuitously. There is no single right way. For it to happen at all requires us to deeply understand who we are. Through self-love, we come to understand our natural flow, and in that flow, our innate talents, strengths, and wisdom becomes more readily available to us.

It's like an artist or athlete tapping into their zone, free from the frame of competition. There is no weight. There is no pressure. No one hits the zone without their heart engaged and fully activated. It feels like the whole universe conspiring to move with us. But the athlete who falls back into her head pops out of the zone. Stay in the zone, and we ascend along the most optimal path to become the best version, the highest vibration, of ourselves.

Growth of this kind does not occur in the suffocating compression and fire of the corporate mindset crucible. Humans under the pressures and stresses of the colonial model aren't like deep deposits of coal destined to turn into diamonds under the weight of millennia. We are more like blades of grass crushed under the weight of a stone.

In other words, we don't need to be broken down in order to build ourselves back up. We don't have to follow rules that so clearly work against us and our evolution. Instead, we can walk the path of the heart and reach our true destination, as we will explore and clarify in Part II.

Part II

ACCESS YOUR HEART

Chapter 4

BREATHE AND
BE WHOLE

s we saw in Part I, choosing the brain-centered corporate mindset means being driven by the outside world. Choosing your heart, however, means being guided by your own internal truths. This is the difference between leading from the brain versus leading from the heart. It is now your choice as to how you want to drive the model of success you live by.

Although the colonial mindset has placed much pressure on you, you can choose to respond to challenging situations, interpersonal conflicts, and systematic struggles from a better place: centered in your heart. This is where you can give yourself permission to love yourself, breathe freely, and lead from your own joyful wisdom. You can choose to respond with insight and a deep knowingness of your own truths, regardless of how others might remain tangled in the fight.

When you choose to lead from your heart, you cultivate the space to know that you have everything you need to do the real work that's necessary to succeed. Growth does not require struggle. It requires peace and stillness deep inside for you to be able to hear your own whispers of wisdom. This inner voice of your heart opens, strengthens, and flows to fruition. This is the foundation of your power. This true sense of real power will begin to supplant the frustrated ruminations of your mind.

BREATH EXERCISE

The journey begins with the breath.

In this book and in our work, we speak a lot about breath. In fact, one of our favorite questions to kick off a coaching session is simply "How are you breathing?" Awareness of breath is powerful and can serve as a strong foundation as we delve deeper into who we are, our self-awareness, and from there begin to understand how we can express and operate more fully in daily life. So, if breath is so important, it is worthwhile for us to pause here for a moment and discuss it.

Much has been written about breath and how vital it is. Groups as varied as swamis, Western medicine physicians, and world-class athletes can all agree on one thing: good breathing is incredibly important. In this book, we invite you to take a breath often, and we will do so again in just a moment. But when we talk about breath, there are two key aspects to consider.

First is the physical. The physical components of breath are something we are all familiar with as we have been doing it since we were born. There is an inhale portion and an exhale portion. But what we often fail to recognize is that both parts start and end by relaxing. As we approach the end of an inhalation, we relax, and then begin the exhalation. When we exhale, as we approach the end of the exhalation, we again relax, and begin our next inhalation. In this way we maintain a never-ending, continuous stream of relaxing. Good breath is done physically in this way, silently, constantly relaxing, and in peace.

The second key aspect of breath is the energetic component. Breath is an indicator of our current state, both externally and internally. When we are at peace, our breath is slow, gentle, and quiet, reflective of the same attributes that constitute peace. When we are agitated, our breath is fast, choppy, and loud, reflective of the attributes that constitute agitation. In this way, our breath tells others where we are. It is also a signal back to ourselves, telling us where we are in mind, body, and spirit.

As compared to other bodily movements and functions, breathing is fairly unique in that it is conducted largely unconsciously, but we also have a great deal of control over it. It is this unique quality of breathing that makes breathwork such a powerful force in gaining deeper insight into ourselves. We can adjust our breath and thereby adjust our signaling to the world and to ourselves as to where we are, and through this awareness, we can put ourselves into a different, more productive state.

Three Deep Breaths

Right now, we will begin our breath exercise by getting into a state of peaceful self-love. To do this, take three long, slow, deep, and cleansing breaths to center yourself in the relevance of your own heart. Inhale and relax, then exhale and relax, slowly, three times. Your very breathing confirms that you are whole and your existence matters deeply. You do this not out of ego, or reward, or because you "need to relax," but only to feel just how deep your love for yourself flows. This is a loving gift you give to yourself, the gift of just a few moments where nothing else matters but you and your love for yourself. When you have completed your three breaths, say aloud, "I love myself."

HEART TALK

Now, sit and explore what it looks like and feels like to be in your own heart with all of your senses activated and dynamically engaged. How have those three mindful breaths changed you, your body, your mind, and your heart? Know that this is you, and this is why we can say with such certainty that you are enough, and you always have been. This is you in your whole self.

You have made the first choice. To carry this wisdom forward, remove any tensions and blocks that take you back into your brain where your fear and ego can run amok. To continue to make the same choice in every breath, in every second of every minute in every hour of every day, we are going to walk you through the shifts from brain talk to heart talk.

As you navigate this journey, you will begin to hear the wisdom of your heart dominate the fear of your ego. You will begin to feel a deep sense of power coming from a peaceful place as it subdues the worry, concern, and anxiety in your brain. It is important that you take note of how you see, hear, and feel the wisdom of your heart reemerge in your consciousness. This will set the new norm for you to understand who you are when you are whole and able to be at your best. From that place, you can then develop accountability, to yourself and to others, to be in that norm more regularly until you are in it all the time.

Shifting from brain to heart is uplifting and liberating as you begin to detach from your connections to the rules of the corporate mindset. The old rules are useless to the journey of evolution and growth that you have now chosen.

Breath by breath, your own heart-centered knowingness and love of self will free you from the expectations and limitations that others have placed upon you. You will leave them to fight their own fitful struggles with the colonial mindset. Fueled by the inner wisdom of your heart, you step aside from the projections of other people's traumas. You walk the path of the leader you are designed to be. That is your purpose in this life. Because you are now moving from heart and not brain, you are able to assume leadership from a place of self-knowing rather than ego. This is truth.

With each choice to love yourself, the knowingness that you were uniquely designed to bring something special to this world becomes more and more clear. In self-love, we are all special beings with amazing hearts that have a brilliant and wonderful light to shine in this world. Knowing this in yourself and giving space to simply honor this truth is the pathway for authentically moving through and showing up in the world.

Your heart will become well versed in how to speak truth to power, far better than your brain ever was or could be. You will no longer require external motivation or attachment to the corporate mindset. Your inner voice offers you a new path motivated by empowerment from the inside out. This is the genesis of real power that serves the common good.

As you breathe through the journey, know that true leadership only requires one thing: authenticity in being you. Your own sense of who you are as a leader in this world emerges from your own heart journey.

Your empowerment as a leader grows in these ways:

1. Learning how to breathe from the depths of your heart, where you know that you are already free.
2. Centering the importance of your own self-love by listening to your inner voice.
3. Doing the work to rediscover your truths so that they might guide you into your personal brand of joyful leadership.

4. Allowing the joy that you feel when you love yourself to be the radiance that you move through the world with, in all that you do.

> Truly, the greatest risk in life is to stay where you already know that you are not in joy.

Humans are designed to grow from within, and this can happen far more readily if we follow the wisdom of our own hearts, or what we call the wisdom of joy. Joy cultivates a path of growth and development in which each person illuminates their own path to becoming the leader they are destined to be. When we lead with joy, notions of success stem from the wisdom of our hearts more than from any title or accolade. Truly, the greatest risk in life is to stay where you already know that you are not in joy.

INTO OUR HEARTS

Nelson Mandela touched upon a key truth, one that many of us may struggle with while mired in the game of the corporate mindset. He said, "There is no passion to be found in playing small, in settling for a life that is less than the one that you are capable of living."

While we may feel that we know this to be true, already constrained in our breath and malnourished in our hearts, it can seem too risky not to play the game that everyone else is playing, even if it is clear to us that no one is truly winning. In fact, few of us are truly passionate about the work we do. Fewer still feel empowered to do the work that we are passionate about. But when we consider what this really means, "settling for a life that is less than the one you are capable of living," how do we even begin to interpret a concept so vast? What would living a life that is equal to the one you are capable of living look like?

For each person, this is different and requires a considerable level of introspection and self-awareness. As we discussed in the previous chapter, there are differences between brain and heart energy, and much of that gets confused and conflated within the corporate mindset. As we begin the process of disengaging from the corporate mindset, we empower our hearts to take over where our brains previously reigned.

SIMPLE TRUTHS

One of the core beliefs in our coaching at The Big Joy Theory is that the path to radical transformation is paved with simple truths. It is essentially an invitation for leaders to stop overcomplicating things. So let us begin with simple truths that pertain to how you see yourself as a leader:

You are what matters most in this world.
You are worth more, and deserving of better,

than the suffering you currently endure,
in the name of success.

If you find that this simple truth acknowledges your daily struggle, we strongly encourage you to continue along this path. If instead you find yourself feeling a bit defensive, we invite you to consider how much more impactful you could be if you were truly set free, no longer bound by the limitations that the corporate mindset has placed upon you. Imagine what more, beyond title and money, you might achieve.

> At heart, we desire to lead for ourselves.

Know that your relationship with yourself, your career, and your life can all be radically transformed, from the inside out, through your heart. It can all be defined by your best qualities, the ones that you already possess and don't need to do anything to gain. You can be truly free of outside influences, manipulations, and corruptions.

Breaking from the old mindset is about reevaluating with fresh eyes. It's not about fighting the industrial complex, "the machine," or "the matrix." In 2021, we witnessed what was termed the "Great Resignation," with thousands of Americans resigning from dead-end jobs, tired of living from paycheck to paycheck. More accurately, we could call it a "Great Awakening" to the realization that in our hearts we are worth more than the colonial mindset tells us. People at all levels want an impactful life authentically grounded in their hearts. This is a simple but major truth of our times. At heart, we desire to lead for ourselves.

Be Authentically You

Authenticity lives inside you. And living a life that is commensurate with your abilities requires you to seek your authenticity first. Moving fast is only good if you are also moving in the right direction. Worry less about trying to advance, and concern yourself more with knowing who you are. Don't give any more time to a process that walks you out of your own heart. Instead, center your energy, concentration, and love on you. Let your own light be the guide to informing your path forward.

Lead from Within

Emboldened from within, it is now safer to go back and name where, when, and how we were socialized out of our hearts. This is why we invite leaders to turn inward and go back to their inner selves. We need to remember who we were when we were young, before we were pressed to conform to the colonial mindset.

We begin our work by unwinding from where we first got off track, when we first chose to leave our hearts and go into our brains. When we look back upon our lives, we can often find a moment, a shadow, a pain, or a trauma that led to that choice. Just like any wound, it can be hard to look at and may be sensitive to the touch. This is okay. Just breathe and remember that you can authentically love yourself.

You don't have to go back and look at old wounds alone. We often coach our clients through this process. You may choose to work with a coach, advisor, or practitioner who can assist you on your journey. For now, it is only important to name the moment that a crack in your humanity was first created, when you shifted out of the wisdom of your heart and moved into your brain. When that happened, you replaced the wisdom of your heart with a whole lot of "stuff" that other people deemed important for you to learn. And it seemed less risky to follow along than remain on a path of your own making.

In a game in which we are judged by what we know, and not how we love, we tend to overthink our way through life. This is where weeds take root and creep between the cracks of our humanity. Along the path of a life trying to meet other people's expectations, we can find ourselves stumbling over these cracks and getting tripped up. This is where we become "not enough" or, possibly, "too much."

To breathe freely is centering, and your center, of course, is your heart.

The cracks formed in our humanity are not of our own making. If we can remember this, then we can fill those cracks with self-love. Sometimes, however, the trauma is too great, and we are not able to stay in our hearts. When this happens, the real tragedy is that we don't recall how to fill the cracks with self-love. Instead, we go stumbling over cracks as if we created them ourselves. And what grows in cracks? Weeds, some so large that they distract us and block our true path. Trying to fight the weeds is a reasonable response, or so it would seem. But too many people get stuck fighting to clear the weeds for a lifetime.

Wouldn't it simply be easier and more effective to just stop fighting the weeds and instead take a breath, look around, and realize that it is not even your garden that you are standing in? Trying to live and lead outside of your own heart walks you out of your garden and deeper into the weeds.

So don't fight. Recognize that the fight is not your purpose or your goal. Your purpose in this world is to be authentically you. Once you see where cracks in your humanity formed, you can navigate your way back to a healing heart. This is why it is critical to maintain and sustain your breath, because to breathe freely is centering, and your center, of course, is your heart.

To address old hurts, all leaders need a better, deeper, and more authentic understanding of who they are in their own humanity. This knowingness alleviates the control that trauma has upon their sense of self. It is like travelling back to before the trauma ever happened, to see and remember who you were before the weeds took root in your world. To remember who you were then allows you to see who others were before their traumas. You begin to see people more as you once saw your classmates as a child, full of wonderment, inquisitiveness, and delight.

For all the right reasons, every leader must be held accountable for their own projections by naming and resolving their own traumas. This is how organizations can more effectively improve the workplace. It is like weeding the organization from all the traumas that people are bringing in and spreading around. Once people more fully address interpersonal traumas, they can step into a new heartset of leadership that centers people back on who they were trying to become in the first place. We come to realize that if we truly want to win at life and feel good about who we are, then we need to come back to ourselves and lead from within.

LAYERS OF HEALING

To embark upon this work of a lifetime, healing must first be done. The first layer of healing lies in the heart. You cannot go around, above, or below this one. You must go through it. It is the only path forward.

Notable feminist author bell hooks (who opted not to capitalize her name, hoping to keep the public's focus on her work) perhaps said it best: "I believe wholeheartedly that the only way out of domination is love."

The journey to self-love can be difficult because it can be blocked by trauma past and present. As we've said, to heal your sense of self-love, you first need to name your trauma. This is hard because most people feel safer hiding from it. In fact, however, the opposite is true. Not naming your trauma is what gives it power over you. It is allowed to lurk around and hide in your body and soul.

Negativity, toxic energy, and trauma receive your lack of calling it out as permission to stay. Hiding from or ignoring your trauma is not safer; it is incredibly dangerous. Trauma can clog your soul and cause depression, anxiety, even psychosis. Depending on the nature of the trauma, it can lead to physical ailments. Even unresolved family trauma can be passed down intergenerationally, affecting our biological, mental, and energetic makeup. Trauma, left unresolved and pushed down into the subconscious, still finds ways to manifest. The link between psychological distress and health outcomes is evident and well-documented.[10]

As you heal the layers of trauma and hurt disrupting your path, we offer these keys to healing:

---

[10] While there are a number of wonderful articles to support this claim, most, in turn, cite what is likely the most famous work demonstrating this concept, van der Kolk, B. A. (2014). *The Body Keeps the Score: Brain, Mind, and Body in the Healing of Trauma.* Viking.

Keys to Healing Leadership

- Call out the toxic energy for what it is, and pinpoint which false rules are blocking your authentic development as a leader.
- Give the weight of your pain back to those who laid it at your soul in the first place.
- Stop fighting against the trauma, as that energy only feeds the fight.
- Turn toward your own heart and honor all the ways in which you have been living and leading from your own self-love.
- Identify and center your lifelong experiences of whole self from childhood onward, where you were operating from the wisdom of your joy within.
- Choose to live and lead from your joy each moment of every day.
- If you need help to do the work, ask for it. Don't let ego stop you from what you are truly capable of.

Back to Your Whole Self

When we experience trauma, often in our childhoods, most of us are not given the power or tools to effectively process our pain. Instead, we process what we can and suppress the rest in order to survive. Over the years, most of us still have not had sufficient resources or space to go back and unpack all that we have suppressed. The toxicity of these early traumas remains embedded deep within us, affecting our thinking, physical health, and energy.

Some of us have the wonderful opportunity to heal our cognitions with a psychologist or find adaptive mechanisms to move forward in our professional lives through coaching. However, if we don't also heal the negatively charged energetic fields that encapsulated and froze our inner child, we are still unable to operate fully from our whole self.

> Your inner critic will be replaced with the wisdom and voice of joy.

It is here that the transformation and transmutation must occur for the truths and wisdoms of our inner children to be turned right side up and right way round. We need to be reunited with our whole selves in a way that heals the breaks in our self-awareness, self-expression, and self-efficacy. This is where we take the time to heal the fissure that formed in our self-confidence when perhaps a teacher told us we wouldn't amount to much; or a parent said we would never make it as an artist; or we were teased by other kids for any number of reasons. Just like a break in a bone that did not mend correctly, that fissure is where your inner child has been waiting for you to return and fully heal and resolve that old trauma.

Beyond that original hurt, your love, light, and wisdom are still, and always have been, relevant in this world. Remember how you breathed before the trauma? It is time to remember how well you led before someone told you that you couldn't. In the wisdom of your own self-love, you will remember just how amazing you were and already are, and your inner critic will be replaced with the wisdom and voice of joy.

So, as we move even further away from the toxic energy of the corporate mindset, releasing the constraints of a system that doesn't allow us to even name our traumas, we eliminate the tensions and blocks that have been keeping us from breathing and resolving these traumas in the first place.

LEAD FROM THE INSIDE

Everywhere, people are fighting: to breathe, to be seen, to get the work done, to not be micromanaged, to succeed through competition as they were taught. The kicker is that in reality, people are not really fighting the machine. They are fighting their own internal conflict and unresolved traumas. They are fighting narratives they took on years before they ever started in their current job, likely before they started any job. They are fighting the weeds that are now overgrown and have come to surround their heart.

So many leaders project their own traumas onto people at work. Those projections trigger others, who then react out of their own trauma. And so it goes. The cycle of trauma that spreads not so silently, sadly unchecked throughout organizations, is the vehicle through which weeds begin to take over the culture. After all, the saying "shit rolls downhill" didn't come from nowhere.

People spend a good portion of time at work projecting their hurts. The hurts go flying in all directions, and we wind up having to protect ourselves from others' projections or avoid them altogether, none of which is very productive for the individual, and certainly not for the organization. Leaders who got lost along their own life path spread their hurt by projecting their traumas onto others in the form of control and constraints.

Control, we tend to understand, if for no other reason than it being pounded into us ever since kindergarten: "Do what I say because I am the parent/teacher/boss!" While most leaders understand that it is inappropriate to say it in quite that way to an adult, for most it would be more honest if they did, wouldn't it? Instead, we teach leaders to say the same thing, but masked in niceness, so we kid ourselves. We pretend that we don't hear all the trauma and oppression within. These "niceties" of leadership are just part of the constraints holding the culture back.

Avoiding conflict is like ignoring the weeds in your garden. You can ignore them all you want, but they will just take over, covering the whole landscape. Allow for that, and any sprouting trees, new plants, or flowers you once had will surely be smothered. This will not work. It is unproductive for individuals and unsustainable for organizations. Companies try to distract their people with gadgets, promos, after-work parties, and "fun" activities, but in the end these tactics all fall short and people are rarely, if ever, fooled.

To access our own authenticity, we can no longer accept pretensions of wearing our "kindness" glasses to avoid confrontation. In the shadows of the organization, it only fuels the fight. In fact, being "kind" is just another way of neglecting, and thereby fueling, the conflict, when the real problem is that people are suffocating in their workplaces and can't breathe.

Take a breath and walk on the brighter side of leadership.

Leaders must address the ways in which they are "managing" or "controlling" the dynamics in the workplace because this is exactly where so much harm is done. Organizations can no longer fake their way to having a healthy ecosystem when the culture is rotten at the core. Instead, we need to start leading from the inside out, with our harms named and healed and our hearts open and ready to lead. We must take off those fake kindness glasses and shed the false truths of the corporate mindset. We need to explore more holistic, universal rules that govern our hearts. To get this process kickstarted, take a breath and walk on the brighter side of leadership.

Rules for the Brighter Side of Leadership

- Everyone is a leader and can lead from wherever they're at.
- There is plenty of room for all leaders at all levels.
- Good organizations build a culture that fits all their leaders.
- Leaders are meant to challenge the status quo.
- Leading through strengths inspires everyone to higher levels of performance.
- Leaders are to always bring their whole selves.
- Conflict is an opportunity.
- Diversity is a strength.

These rules are life-giving. They have breath in them. They create space for organizations to grow with the talents, strengths, wisdom, and joy of all their leaders, present, past, and future. There is accountability and wholeness beyond the ways people are currently categorized and siloed in their work. Diversity is centered as a foundational strength, not an output that leaders hope to achieve, one day, maybe, when the time is right. We reconceptualize challenges for the opportunities that they are. In this frame, we remove the struggle of work and instead embrace it as evolution, individually and collectively. Notice too that these rules line up perfectly but are near exact opposites to the rules of the corporate mindset presented in Chapter 2 under "The Rules." We offer them side by side in Chapter

4 under "Rules to Shift Mindset of Leadership." This is what the brighter side of leadership sounds like, outside of corporate mindset models of leadership.

Leaders whose hearts are heavy from trying to climb within the corporate mindset to reach their own breath often feel liberated by simply reading these rules. Many exhale the weight they have been carrying and begin to sit back into their hearts for the first time in years. Like most wisdoms of the heart, they have known these truths for some time, but it is so refreshing to hear them aloud, confirmed in the present time and space.

In our work at The Big Joy Theory, we often encounter leaders who say they believe in these rules, deeply, but don't know how to live by them, especially in the way the system is designed today. Leaders trapped inside the old mindset will say, "That all sounds nice, but there are real constraints and hard decisions we have to make here." Some who have already compromised their sense of self are fearful of letting go of the old way. It got them this far, right?

Perhaps you feel similarly, that there's just not enough time for all this, or that it's not real leadership because leadership is about getting shit done. To all such leaders, we say that it sounds like you are not yet breathing. You've come this far on the path, but you still have cold feet. Take a breath and know that you are enough. Stop trying to lead with your brain when your heart is so much more powerful and productive. The wisdom that you seek comes from your heart, which is the mechanism of your joy within. Have faith that you will address even the most hard-nosed business metric far better and more comprehensively than anything you are currently able to concoct using your brain.

Now breathe. On the brighter side of leadership, take a long, deep breath in and out, releasing any tensions that you may be harboring in your body. Along this part of the journey, our intention is to get back to our whole selves, so the removal of tensions and blocks in your way is critical. If this is such a block, acknowledge it as such. Breathe on it until its tight grip upon you loosens. With each breath, you are gradually releasing a lifetime of trauma. This is the healing that brings liberation from the old mindset. We must eliminate the barriers that have been preventing us from loving ourselves and operating in the wisdom of our hearts.

As you continue on this journey, remember that you don't have to compromise your sense of self in order to survive anything in life —not work, not your family, not your cultural struggles. Compromising ourselves is actually the greatest burden, and here's why:

Compromising yourself...

- leaves less air for you to breathe;
- weighs down your soul;
- burdens your loved ones with managing all the manifestations of your unnamed traumas; and
- is, in fact, the biggest risk you can take if you ever hope to do more than just survive.

The people we have locked out of leadership and left in their own struggles without support are hurting. We each need to find our way back to our own authentic path to becoming who we are designed to be. This is why we must take the time to find peace, breathe, and fully decompress and unfold on the journey of reintegrating our hearts into our leadership.

Centered in Your Whole Self

From a place of whole self, know that as you navigate your personal journey into the brighter side of leadership, all kinds of people will feel threatened by it. All too many have been tricked into thinking that love, wisdom, and joy are a threat to the old order and their place in it. When this occurs, remain centered in your whole self, knowing that you cannot afford to love yourself any less or try to accommodate someone who doesn't know how to love themselves. You are worth so much more than that.

Leaders we've advised at The Big Joy Theory tell us that as they grow into their true selves—"just breathing and being me"—things gradually become easier in the workplace. Here are just a handful of examples of what leaders have told us about finding their way within the brighter side of leadership:

- "I am free."
- "I am motherfucking magic."

- "I have already conquered this."
- "The old way wasn't me. It never has been."
- "My dreams don't have to be a fantasy."
- "I know how to do this."
- "If I keep this stress for any amount of time, then I lose that time."
- "I just need to be on the timeline of my soul."
- "I am way further ahead than I thought."
- "Shame is the accountability of self-hate."
- "Not trusting myself and listening to myself in times of transition strips the joy of my evolution."
- "I am already healing intergenerational curses."
- "Joy is the nucleus of it all, and I want to keep it at the center because it's just easier and healthier."
- *[We are reserving this space for you. Insert yours here.]*

This is exactly where we are headed. Through breath opening to heart, you discover that all you seek in yourself and the world around you is there waiting for you. In fact, it's been there all along, the truths your heart has known since you were a child. This is why we need to name and process our childhood traumas.

When you name and process your traumas,

- you become unwilling to compromise yourself anymore within the corporate mindset;

- you breathe freely, and knowing that you are whole, you are ready to tap into the wisdom of your heart;
- you engage in the virtuous action that your heart calls forward; and
- you continually build a life that calls for constant account-ability to yourself, your self-love, and your joy.

True leaders seek balance, peace, and harmony. The source resides within each of us. That which you seek is right here, in your own heart, embedded in your own self and how you communicate with yourself. It's therefore vital that our own "self-talk" be fundamentally informed by the wisdom of joy rather than the critical voice of the old colonial mindset.

It is a choice to live on the brighter side of leadership. It always has been. It always will be. You just need to choose from your heart. It's time to start living and working with new joyful rules to shift the mindset of leadership.

RULES TO SHIFT MINDSET OF LEADERSHIP

Corporate Mindset	The Brighter Side of Leadership
Leadership is top-down.	Everyone is a leader and can lead from wherever they're at.
There is little room at the top for leaders.	There is plenty of room for leaders at all levels.
Good employees fit into the culture of the organization.	Good organizations build a culture that fits all their employees as leaders.
Employees are to toe the company line.	Leaders are to challenge the status quo.
Fear and stress are good motivators for performance.	Leading through strengths inspires everyone to higher levels of performance.
Work comes first; personal stuff stays at home.	Leaders always bring their whole selves to their work.
Conflict is a problem.	Conflict is an opportunity.
Diversity is a burden.	Diversity is a strength.

NO FIGHTING IN THE GARDEN

In the garden of your heart, there is one universal and unbreakable rule: no fighting in the garden.

The key to always abiding by this rule is to lead through your sense of self-love. There is no fear when you receive the life experiences that have shaped you through the lens of self-love. Even the traumatic experiences in life become more effectively recentered, not as a reflection upon you and who you are or were but as a reflection upon the person or people who hurt you and caused you the trauma in the first place. You won't have the burden of their toxic energy anymore. You needn't feel guilt or shame for what is past.

No matter your age when trauma was laid upon you, it no longer has to burden you or stand in your way. It's time to clear the weeds and bloom to your relevance in this world.

In this way, we remove the fight from the garden. We quiet the mind so the heart can be heard. We pluck the weed so the flower may bloom. Abiding by this rule is vital for the long-term success of our evolution into joy. Stumbles may occur, especially when triggered by the same people who originally hurt us, but our actions will come from heart and joy, not fear and self-doubt. This is the difference between getting stuck in the weeds of brain and travelling the clear path of a joyful heart.

LEADING WELL

Leading from your truest sense of who you are, with your self-love fully intact and the wisdom of your joy completely engaged, is leading well. It is the surest path. You don't have to climb ladders. Your most meaningful impact in the world comes when you are safe enough, whole enough, and free enough to bring the alchemy of your soul to the world.

> Your leadership will be inspirational.

You will be free to engage as you see fit, able to hold yourself accountable for meaningful engagement in your work. It is much more fun, productive, and sustainable to live and lead in this way. Your leadership will be inspirational.

Often, when working with startup clients, we find that they are heavily oriented toward the big payday at the end of the startup journey—the multimillion-dollar acquisition or IPO. This is clearly and deeply rooted in brain energy. Hearts don't care much about IPOs. So we simply tell them, "We can't guarantee that you'll have a billion-dollar exit, but the greatest likelihood of such an outcome will come from performing at your best. And to perform at your best, you need to be tapped into your authenticity, your self-love, and the wisdom of your heart. So, even if your real goal here is the giant pile of money at the end of the rainbow (which, of course, it isn't), tapping into your heart, weeding your garden, and finding authenticity through self-love is still the most productive path."

The same can be said for even the most brain-oriented goals you might have for yourself. While we'd prefer that you leave those goals and reorient on heart-centered goals, simply ask yourself what the most productive path to those brain goals would look like. How might you increase the likelihood of achieving those goals through your heart instead of risking everything by continuing to pursue them from your brain?

So, for you, dear reader, the work is simply this: be whole.

To be whole, you must find your authentic voice. You must tap into your heart and understand your truths as compared to those that others have placed upon you. You must breathe. You must love yourself enough to do the work of reorienting yourself to the truths in your heart. This is how you will unlock yourself from the corporate mindset.

Creative Leadership

Unshackled, you become a free agent, no longer beholden to a degree, a boss, a career, or an organization. People are designed to lead from a place of creativity and innovation, necessary for our individual and collective evolution. Healthy mechanisms of leadership liberate people to be their best, most creative selves.

When people feel boxed in and aren't free to create, human innovation stops. This is why humanity must shift away from the old colonial rules. Without heart wisdom, society is droughted and famished like a garden where no rain falls. Beyond all the man-made divisions and silos of the corporate world exists the potential for leadership to flourish at every level of the workplace. Leadership isn't created through "followership." It takes creative expression throughout an organization to attain the highest and truest standards of success.

SELF-EVIDENT TRUTH

We've known these truths long before modern corporate life was a reality. Born of the highest human ideals, the United States Declaration of Independence famously declares, "We hold these truths to be self-evident, that all [people] are created equal...with certain unalienable Rights, that among these are Life, Liberty and the pursuit of Happiness."

This is certainly true and has been for a long time. We are entitled to move unfettered by the imposition of others. We are free to live, lead, and love. If not now, when? Everything you truly need is already inside of you. Leading from the heart is your unalienable right.

This is why finding your breath is so important. You need your breath to pump your blood and beat your heart. To impact the world, we must learn to breathe and be whole. Listen to your heart. Live its wisdom.

Chapter 5

WISDOM AND BRILLIANCE
OF THE HEART

The process of reestablishing connection to our hearts is where we build trust and faith in our own internal wisdom. Yet in a world so driven by brain energy, we can all fall prey to listening more to our brains than our hearts—it seems like the prudent thing to do. All too many of us wind up trusting that which is outside of us, failing to trust our own internal hearts or, as some might call it, our "gut" instincts.

The key to differentiating heart energy from brain energy is to simply identify where it is coming from. If a thought, feeling, or decision is rooted in fear, competition, anxiety, or anger, you can be sure it is coming from your brain. It is a response to outside stimuli, the body trying to survive in some form or fashion. Any thought that falls into the fight-or-flight response is all brain. Conversely, if action or decision comes from a place of calm awareness, self-love and expression, and genuine affection for yourself or others, then it is your heart speaking.

Heart is what feels freeing, empowering, like open space and opportunity. Conversely, the brain is limiting, diminishing, often adversarial and judgmental. Brain is the organ of doubt and self-doubt. You may doubt the teachings on this page, or you may doubt your own needs, feelings, or sense of self. When we feel threatened, the brain fights for relevance. It doesn't want to let go. Brain is all ego. What it needs most is for us to assert our individual identities. Brain is self-involved and self-interested. On the other hand, the heart is empathetic; it reaches out and wants what's best for the community, whether a family or an organization. Heart is generous and open.

What is particularly fascinating about listening to your heart is that once you start doing it regularly, you begin to see just how vast and expansive the wisdom of your heart truly is. We often diminish heart-based decisions as wishy-washy or soft, not fully thought through. But nothing could be further from the truth. The heart can make the most concrete, complex, and sophisticated decisions without the need for spreadsheets because it factors in the widest range of objective and subjective information, inclusive of both facts and feelings.

We've all heard about "emotional intelligence," which is, of course, seated in the heart, and the value it brings to individuals, leadership, and organizations. The heart weighs concrete information along with the subjective perspectives of many players, including customers and clients, coworkers and company leaders, vendors, and all company stakeholders. The heart has a way of sorting the most relevant data through our own intuition all while we breathe.

The Rational Heart

The idea that you should trust the wisdom of your own heart, above and beyond the data of the physical world, has been weaponized as selfish and dangerous by the corporate mindset. The old order wants to sustain its dominance, so it questions the sanity of the heart. The brain-centered colonial mindset operates out of fear and ego, so it condemns heart-based thinking as irresponsible, irrational, and soft.

The old mindset exists only to feed itself and preserve its own power and authority. Brain energy has so diminished the wisdom of the heart that individuals no longer know how to trust their inner voice. Yet, the heart is where knowledge of the brain is combined with intuition to illuminate real wisdom. From wisdom comes peace and joy. So nothing could be more sane, rational, and practical than listening to our hearts.

THREE CORE PRINCIPLES OF THE
HEART IN LEADERSHIP

To aid you in identifying the wisdom of your own heart, we'll look at what we call "three core principles of the heart in leadership." These principles may not sound like grand revelations, but they are incisive and cut to the chase.

Notice your reactions to them. If you react with thoughts or feelings that say these truths are wrong or dumb, take a measure: are you responding from brain or heart? Take a breath and explore further.

If, on the other hand, the principles feel true and empowering, your heart is engaged. Keep going with that and wonder what else your heart might be noticing. If you feel these principles are too simple, obvious, or mundane, perhaps your heart has already known them to be true for a long time. If that is the case, then simply consider how wise and sophisticated your heart must truly be, and what more might be in there that you have yet to hear.

Principle 1: The Path to Radical Transformation
Is Paved with Simple Truths

The first core principle to understand in our evolution into joy is that some of the grandest movements in the world originate from simple truths. We began a discussion of simple truths in the last chapter with the simplest of truths: your relevance in the world.

Simple truths, such as the relevance of each individual, have contended with power structures that have denied the individual throughout human history. For example, the US Civil War was about hearts speaking the simple truth that humans, regardless of skin color, should not be slaves. That's pretty simple, and to any rational person, it's an unquestionable truth. However, at the time, a powerful colonial mindset clung fiercely to the status quo in the name of "states' rights," economic convenience, racism, and white supremacy.

More than 600,000 Americans had to die in a struggle of stubborn, self-absorbed brain energy against a simple, rational, moral truth of the heart. An obvious, simple truth led to a profound transformation of social dynamics, politics, and economics in ways that have left indelible marks on the country more than a century and a half later.

In the corporate world, a simple truth continues to go unnoticed: we are each endowed with leadership capacity. This truth is denied in order to bolster the bestowed "privilege" of leadership reserved for only the chosen few. These are the few elites who have the "credentials" and inclination to jump through all the corporate hoops to the top. Leadership wonks love to debate whether leadership is innate or taught, as if it must be an all-or-none proposition.

The simple truth is that the capacity for leadership stems from the confluence of both knowledge and intuition resulting in wisdom seated in the heart. Our best leaders know how to lead with wisdom born of joy. This is an art that can be honed and mastered over time through awareness and practice. Leadership is both innate and learned. And we are all designed to lead in some meaningful way. We just have to look behind the titles and around the noise to understand the full potential for leadership.

These are simple truths: slavery is evil, and leadership is a quality of being human. We hold these truths to be self-evident.

Principle 2: Authentic Leaders Are Led by Their Collective Impact, Not Their Ego

The second core principle of the heart goes deeper into the concept of leadership and how to identify authentic leadership. Authentic leaders have a wide breadth of understanding because they rely on wisdom born of learned knowledge and intuition. They have capacity for love and self-love beyond any ego identity.

When authentic leaders become self-actualized and can fully realize their potential, there is a natural evolution to lead on behalf of others. Authentic leadership is not about title, salary, or control of a massive budget. Those metrics are designed to reward the ego and keep people locked into the corporate mindset. To manifest leadership potential in the workplace, people need to be released from this linear illusion of success.

Authentic leadership is about the depth of impact centered in our shared, collective humanity. It's the kind of leadership that can shift the thinking of a large group of people. It's a way of living and leading that in its simplicity inspires others to rise to new challenges. The key is that all leaders have their part, and all parts are truly equal in their importance. Leadership at its core is about the continued co-creation of our humanity.

We've all heard stories of leaders who played the corporate game, high-level executives who had tremendous egos, power, and influence in their sphere, and made a bunch of money, yet were miserable. They rose through the ranks of other ego-led leaders to illustrious careers and retired with golden parachutes, multiple ex-spouses, estranged children, and long-lost friends. It's a sad story of some genuinely good people who were misled by data from the outside, while never connecting to the resources of their own hearts.

In our work as executive coaches, we meet many leaders like these while they still have a chance to change. Some are resistant, but they all want desperately to change because they know that they are missing the joy of leading. They are hungry for a deeper impact and more honest, loving, and truthful connections with their fellow human beings.

Tapping into the heart provides a much clearer and more productive path. It lends itself to great transformation, collective impact that can benefit entire communities and even countries. It's the measure by which we can evaluate the worth of a leader, one who is accountable to their own heart and the hearts of others. Think Abraham Lincoln; think Martin Luther King; think Mahatma Gandhi; think Joan of Arc.

Principle 3: Leadership Exists to Inspire the Self and Others Beyond Their Limitations

The third core principle of the heart goes further inward to leadership from a management and team perspective. Just as we can identify authentic leadership from its collective impact and absence of ego, we can also identify true leadership from how it inspires others. Until you have inspired the people you lead, you have not truly led.

There are countless memes and pithy phrases about the differences between management and leadership. But these distinctions are fundamental to an organization's overall success.

Management is about corralling and keeping in good working order what is already there. You can manage a bunch of machines whirring around to keep them stamping out widgets. But no matter how well you manage those machines, they'll never do more than what they were built to do. They'll just work and do their job, and nothing more. Sadly, as a function of the limited view of the Industrial Revolution and the corporate mindset, this has been the expectation of most managers when it comes to both machines and people.

Leadership, on the other hand, is about setting a course for others to follow. From the perspective of the corporate mindset, people follow from a fixed position behind the leader. Yet, when we consider leading from the perspective of heart, leaders encourage growth and innovation, not just in a company's products and services but in its people. The heart-oriented leader wants to unleash the full potential and imagination of their team members. If someone blows past the leader with a new concept, the leader is energized, interested, and supportive, not threatened. In the heart sense, leadership isn't competition; it's inspiration.

The old mindset falsely assumes a single trajectory of leading, usually based on title or money. Instead, the unleashing of leadership allows for countless directions of innovation and growth. Those who are now freed through the authentic leader's guidance can go firing off in every direction, following their truest passions, operating from their own hearts, and bringing all of themselves to the work. In this manner, companies and their people become fully actualized in all sorts of ways that even the most brilliant brain could never have foreseen while enmeshed in the corporate mindset.

Authentic leadership promotes a personal accountability and responsibility to lead so well that others are inspired to move beyond the forces that have held them back. To lead well is to inspire people for all the right reasons. Authentic leaders aren't looking for titles or money; they take their own inspiration from the collective endeavor of jobs well done and mutual growth. They aren't self-promoters. Instead, they seek to elevate and advance the people they work with. They open and expand the field of opportunity for others to lead, authentically and from heart.

YOUR HEART IS THE VOICE OF
YOUR EMPOWERMENT

The three core principles of the heart are fairly simple. But simple truths can bring great transformation in leadership that impact an organization and free others beyond their limitations. When we take them to heart and live by them as profound truths, rather than simple leadership sound bites, they can yield sophistication of action and profound outcomes.

> There is only one path to being a failure: you trying to be anyone other than you.

The simple truths that Nelson Mandela lived by and advocated brought enormous change and collective impact to South Africa. His leadership inspired multitudes worldwide and freed generations beyond their limitations. Leading from a place of humility and not competition proved to be extremely effective in Mandela's lifetime and beyond.

There is only one path to being a failure: you trying to be anyone other than you. Attempting to live and work under the old rules of the colonial mindset devalues our self-worth as individuals. The outcome for so many of us is sadness, anger, regret, and shame.

When we stray from the critical truths of the core principles of the heart, the heart knows it.

The role of the ego in dominating others has reached a critical point in human culture. On social media, anyone who can project their voice with confidence is taken as putting forward truths. However, the projection of forcefulness should not suffice for people to say, "Well, that must be true." The true measure of value in expressed opinion is whether it lifts people humanely and inspires good will.

This is something that has unfortunately been lost in leadership. Competition in the blogosphere does not inspire the collective good but rather weaponizes people and groups, teams and organizations, against one another. Competition breeds fear of losing, and fear of losing feeds the scarcity mindset. Our most transformative leaders put ego aside and embrace very simple yet powerful truths that inspire others to work for our collective social and physical well-being.

Living and working from the heart is the place from which inspiration and empowerment flows. Simply consider that you might already be enough with your own unique talents, strengths, passions, and dreams. Your most authentic self is waiting to be realized and put to action.

Unsound Sound Bites

The powers that be say that if you want to be a good leader, then you are going to have to learn to be tough and fight your way to the top. "Strengths and growth only come through continuous effort and struggle," says American self-help guru Napoleon Hill.

This worldview is supported by age-old mantras like "when the going gets tough, the tough get going" or "tough times don't last; tough people do." Even the old classic "no pain, no gain," which we've all heard countless times, is actually a nearly 2,000-year-old phrase. It comes from a second-century rabbi who, roughly translated, said, "according to the pain is the gain." It referred to the spiritual development that comes from doing what God requires. But that spiritual sound bite found favor in the 1980s to sell aerobics videos. It is marketing fluff, not truth. You cannot possibly be setting your life model to the catchy taglines that were used to sell VHS cassettes or falsely justify our ancestors' suffering.

For the current leaders of corporate America, these mantras are still alive and well, stirring deep within their leadership values. As a result, the power dynamics embedded into the game, whether we believe in them or not, still require us to perform in accordance with such antics. So people trudge on in the name of doing what they have to do to appease their boss, get their paycheck, and simply survive. That is not leading. Heck, it is barely living.

HEART LEADS BY EXAMPLE

Now that you see the game for what it is, you can also see that fighting it only feeds its power. The command structure of the corporate mindset is utterly invested in its own relevance and imperative to stay alive. Fighting against a system based on supremacy only signals it to dig in deeper. It will simply interpret your protestations as weakness. However, we don't do nothing. What we do is project a better way by example.

When you understand your own self-love, inner light, and the wisdom of your joy, you will know that you can't tear down a system designed to keep people fighting. Instead, you can help cultivate a new system, despite those who will cling to the failing infrastructure of a civilization already lost in its own devolution. Rather than being drawn into the fight, turn toward your own evolution and don't look back. Just keep going into joy.

When leaders return to the truths and wisdom that empowered them before trauma settled in, they are reinvigorated and inspired. It is always a miraculous sight to behold. They come to realize that no one really needs to struggle to grow. We don't need to suffer in the name of becoming better. We can let go of the old, learned patterns of struggle wrought with pain.

> You must choose to love yourself over continuing to fight.

The corporate mindset defines all change as risk. However, the greatest risk in life is to not choose to be our most authentic selves. We need to stop fighting, reject the battlefield, and lead from a place of joy and self-acceptance. In this manner, we become a role model for our family, coworkers, friends, and all we may encounter.

So many of the battles that people are fighting have already been fought and won by our ancestors. One of our favorite things to do with leaders stuck in the fight is to ask them directly if they think they're going to do a better job than all those who came before. For example, to the person fighting for racial justice, we ask, "Do you really think you're going to do better than Martin Luther King, Malcolm X, Frederick Douglass, Harriet Tubman, Sojourner Truth, James Baldwin, Maya Angelou, W.E.B. Du Bois, and so many others? Haven't they already said it all? What do you really intend to add to what they've already shared?"

Those who have come before us have already done the work and said everything that needs to be said. That some people choose to still not listen, is their choice to stay in the fight. To stay ignorant and woefully behind. But for you to keep fighting the same fight is also a choice. What we need to do now with the profound inheritance of all those great leaders is to breathe new, joyful living into the legacy that they have already built. You must choose it, deep in your soul.

You must choose to love yourself over continuing to fight on the battlefield in survival mode. You will have to stop seeking attention as a warrior, a superwoman, the smartest person in the room, a caregiver, a black sheep. You need to breathe that all out and inhale fresh, revitalizing air. The old roles are not grounded in self-love or informed by the wisdom of your joy. They are warring roles that only distract you from your own evolution. They are roles constructed by trauma, not by your joyful heart and internal truths.

AUTHENTIC LEADERSHIP
OF THE HEART

When the standard of working against our own grain is removed from the notion of achieving success, people begin to relax and breathe. In our own work, we have seen that when people embrace simple principles of the heart, they are able to lead with authenticity and truly harvest the fruits of labor. They are happy to share the gifts of their hearts.

We cannot advance society through a scarcity mindset. It is no longer sustainable. At best we will have small wins for a few and big losses for many. That is the very nature of competition. Only a few get to win, and we see it every day. Even if you try to spread out the wins, as millennial parents and teachers attempted to do by handing out participation trophies, others will insist that you are spoiling, softening, or corrupting the next generation. So, we compete. We busy ourselves in the fight over what winning really means. Meanwhile, those who have already won reap the rewards, and the rest keep on losing. Society doesn't benefit from this model.

However, if leaders live and lead with authenticity, then they win at being themselves, and it inspires others to pursue winning at being authentically themselves. No competition needed. Only celebration, as each human being becomes the best version of themselves. Lifting the traditional frames of competition allows for more space. In that open space, you can more readily feel the various pathways to becoming a leader. You can be a creative leader who inspires others to create in their own best way. It only takes being the best version of yourself and leading with a joyful heart.

We need to stop thinking that the winner with the most is also somehow the best and the most glamorous. Why does the media give us regular updates as to who the richest person in the world is? Does it matter if Jeff Bezos is now richer than Elon Musk or Bill Gates? These are simply distractions of the corporate mindset. We can no longer allow ourselves to be bamboozled by those who look the right way or have the right title or own the most stuff or work out of the biggest office. Instead, we need to strive for wisdom, living and leading with open hearts to have the most impact in our lives. There are so many ways to win simply by being our authentic selves.

Perhaps none of this is really new to you. You've likely thought about these things yourself in quiet moments. Those thoughts, those truths, are the sound of your heart speaking to you. Recognize and embrace it when it happens. If the core principles of leadership discussed in this chapter ring true for you, stick with them. Remain curious about the truths your heart holds. The world around you is eager to share with you, and it is waiting for you to share your own heart's wisdom and brilliance.

Chapter 6

LOVE YOURSELF

You are designed to love yourself and breathe freely into the wisdom of your joy. How could you have been born to do anything else? Your love, light, and joy are the mechanisms of evolution that will guide you on your leadership journey. It is wonderfully simple and yet so wonderfully complex!

LOVE AS THE
FOUNDATION OF JOY

There is simplicity in just following your joy. It is powerful and even disruptive in a positive way for a world so lost and disconnected. However, because the ways in which we love ourselves are so plentiful and our breath so unique, the ways in which our inner light illuminates our own wisdom of joy are highly tailored for each individual leader. This is really a pivotal concept to center on because it gives the ultimate power to you. It is not part of the one-size-fits-all model of leadership that touts five steps to doing this or that, and eight things that the best leaders do, and so on.

This is where complexity enters. There may be some generalizable trends, but each and every bit of progress along your path is specific to you. You can look outside for ideas, but they must always make it through your own filters of truth, breath, love, wisdom, and joy. Taking anything outside of yourself as gospel, without such filtering, skips the most important part, the evaluation of its alignment with who you actually are. So, it becomes a choice: do you want to walk in your own shoes or keep trying to walk in others' worn-out soles?

We do this filtering when it is blatantly necessary. For example, not many of us take leadership notes from the playbooks used by monsters of history, such as Attila the Hun, Hitler, or Idi Amin. Yet we opt to listen with ears wide open to the PhD from a notable university espousing antiquated leadership tropes.

The point is, if you listen to your heart instead of those old, tired tropes, you will get where you want to go faster and easier. Instead of wearing heavy combat boots, you can choose to be light on your feet. Love is the foundation for leadership, and without it, we are putting at considerable risk the very help we want to offer, the passion driving our work, and the impact we can have in the world.

SELF-LOVE

As adults, we hear and even talk about the importance of self-love, but we rarely put it into real action. We seem to understand that self-love is important, and even a sacred truth, when our children are young and first learning the complexities of life. But we continually fail to center love of self in how we educate children in school or in how we learn about work and success. So, self-love falls out of our consciousness during our most formative years.

Yet all is not lost, because self-love is incredibly resilient. It can persist and reemerge with even the slightest attention. So, you are invited to think back, right now, to just how much you loved yourself when you were little. Make certain that you go back far enough to before someone told you that being you was not enough, before some trauma interrupted your innate awareness of how to love yourself.

Recall that you didn't need any special skills to be exuberant and curious about each new day. You knew enough about who you were, what you liked and didn't like, when you were hungry or tired. You even knew when you needed a hug and were more than happy to ask for one. You were clear about who you felt good around and who you didn't want to be around. You knew who you loved and who loved you.

Unfortunately, in "growing up," we were somehow socialized out of loving ourselves. We took on worry and concern about whether we were enough, or ever would be. How old were you when you first began to compare yourself to others? That comparison was the beginning of you reorienting your center from one of self-love to one of ego in the name of competition. Over time, the notion of who we are as competitors sufficiently turns us backward in our own self-esteem, confidence, and self-image. For many it becomes difficult to even remember what it felt like to make decisions from a place of self-love and not trying to keep up with the Joneses. This is how the power of self-love turns from a primary function of our evolution into a so-called "soft skill" that we would be squeamish about listing at even the very bottom of our resumes.

Fully Certified in Your Own Self-Love

How would the world shift if we were less shy about naming and centering love in leadership? Leaders find it hard enough to talk about who they are as people in their professional lives. During the COVID-19 pandemic, as many of us transitioned to working from home, we learned a little something about how we could tear down the barriers between the personal and professional. Our work lives just barged through our front doors and plopped down in our living rooms. It took the full force of a worldwide pandemic, with millions of people dying, for us to even begin to try to get comfortable seeing our colleagues in their personal lives, as humans with homes and kids. And "Look at that! They have a puppy!"

We may have known our workmates were parents, but we'd never met their children, or if we did, it was in a stilted and structured circumstance. We didn't see them during our weekly strategy meeting, running gleefully across the room screaming in joy, possibly without pants. We may have known that a couple of our coworkers had dogs, cats, or other pets, but we never thought we'd see those pets lounging on a couch or barking to be fed. These are just a few facets of who we are as people. There is so much more to know about who each of us truly is in our daily lives, in our hearts. The pandemic shifted us from our safe spaces to a place of vulnerability where we couldn't hide our shared humanity from others as easily as we could at the office.

> Life is about becoming your truest self. You will have won at life once you win at being you.

Think back to taking home that very first report card to your parents. Now imagine that instead of a teacher scoring you on reading or math according to some state-regimented learning standard, it was a report tracking your capacity to demonstrate self-love. Crazy, right? It is so unfathomable because our world is so fascinated by obtaining success through competing with others in what purports to be highly measurable ways. It seems so "pie in the sky" to even consider self-love as a worthy indicator of development and progress. But something inside each of us goes, "Hey, that would have been amazing! I would have loved to be seen for the ways that I loved myself. I would have turned out so different." And yet we do nothing to make any of that a reality outside of our imaginations.

When asked about who they would have become had they been allowed to continue to love themselves, most leaders we work with say things like, "I would have become an artist." They talk about everything from dancing to world travel, writing a book, starting a business, never attending college, and staying in better touch with childhood friends.

Imagine that at your next annual performance review, you were asked to present the many ways in which you demonstrated a higher capacity for making key decisions from a place of self-love. Still ridiculous, huh? Maybe. But what is actually ridiculous is that notions of self-love are seen as nonessential to our development or to leading well. Remember that life is about becoming your truest self. You will have won at life once you win at being you.

However, you may not yet be in a place to put your faith in self-love and the wisdom of your inner child. So we're going to walk you through a few exercises to see that such fundamental truths are not just held by your inner child but by you as a fully grown adult. We'll explore several concepts and activities that touch upon these truths and motivate heart-endorsed action that flows naturally from self-love.

EXERCISE 1: What Really Matters

To begin, let's take a big step back from all the day-to-day nonsense. Breathe it all out, and as you find your center, think about the things that really, and we mean *really*, matter.

To be clear, money does not matter: money is an outcome. Achieving some measurable goal, like a promotion or running a marathon, does not matter; those are outcomes as well. What *really* matters are things internal to you. If you take great care of yourself and your surroundings, money will come, promotions will come, marathons will be run.

With that in mind, we've given you space to list up to eight things internal to you that really matter in your life. Simply name as many that come to mind.

_____

_____

_____

_____

Okay. Well done. Take another breath and consider how making these choices felt. What did you feel as you came up with the first thing on your list? Were you breathing comfortably? Did you give yourself space and time to think about it? Did you judge yourself by how many things you listed or how long it was taking you?

Whatever your experience, simply note it for now. All of it is good. Just recognize it as your own personal experience and consider ways in which you could center love when it comes to what really matters in your life. Many leaders who've done this exercise name things such as making sure they eat and sleep well. That makes sense; we are biological creatures, and we have biological needs to function well. Leaders also reference things like having positive relationships with loved ones and/or with God. Again, this makes sense. Sometimes we get responses such as just stopping to enjoy life for a moment and breathing freely. Once again, no real surprises here.

Now, revisit your list, and ask yourself what connects all the things you listed? What is the singular theme, phrase, or idea that links all of them together? If you had to take your whole list and narrow it down to one concept, what would it be?

This can be tough, so take the time you need.

And now, for the big reveal. Like a magician, we will reveal to you your answer: *self-love.*

All the things you listed can almost certainly be understood as different aspects of your unique and individual expression of self-love. These are things that you would naturally do if self-love was important to living and leading well in this world. You want to do them, and you want the time and space from the people in your life —your family, friends, even your boss—to do them. What if those same people even celebrated the ways in which you were choosing to love yourself each and every day? Imagine how different your annual review would look. You might not even dread those one-on-one meetings with your boss anymore! But let's take it even further and go all the way to checking in with your own sense of self-love.

EXERCISE 2: From Ego to Self-Love

Since the first page of this book, we've been pulling apart the concepts of ego and self-love. By now you have a pretty good handle on these, so take a look at the scale below, which runs from Ego (-100) to Self-Love (+100).

Now, take another deep cleansing breath. When you're ready, consider where you would place yourself on this scale based on how you currently express what is in your heart. If you feel you operate out of your heart all the time, fully expressed in self-love as we've been discussing, give yourself a score nearer to the +100 mark. If, on the other hand, you recognize how you often oper-ate out of your brain, expressing from ego rather than self-love, give yourself a score closer to the -100 mark. To be clear, this isn't a test with passing grades but an opportunity to honestly notice where you are right now. We're just looking to be genuine here and level-set with ourselves. Do your best not to judge the score you give yourself, whatever it may be.

On average, to what extent do you feel that you are currently operating out of Ego (i.e., brain) or Self-Love (i.e., heart)?

EGO ------------------- 0 -------------- **SELF-LOVE**
-100   +100

Note that you can also use this same scale to rate others. But if you do, please be certain to honor that everyone is on a journey of coming into their own self-love, even your family members, your boss, your coworkers, your friends, or those who may have hurt you. This scale is a measure that can allow you to see your own heart and the hearts of others more effectively in a new way.

What was your number? Remember, this number is not a judgment. To even judge it would be to go into ego. The very thought of "I'm great because my number is X" or "I'm bad because my number is Y" is classic brain energy, so ignore it. This is an opportunity for you to finally name where you are on your journey of self-love, period. And we all start somewhere. Now you know where you are, and speaking it out loud allows you to reclaim the journey of your heart. The invitation is for you to now focus your heart on closing the gap between the number that you named and being in self-love all the time. This invitation is not just for today or tomorrow. It is an invitation that is open to your heart for the rest of your life. This is the work of being in joy.

Now, revisit your list of important things from the previous exercise. Take a few minutes to think of two or three things from that list that you would like to start working on, beginning tomorrow. Not because you need to achieve or because you're going to show us how badass you are at being in self-love. But simply because you desire to create more space to lead from your own heart. Remember, we didn't create your list; you did. So, this isn't our homework for you. This is you, as a grown adult, being accountable to you and your heart.

With all this in mind, have a look at the next exercise.

EXERCISE 3: Doing for Self-Love

Take another cleansing breath or two. Recenter your-self in your heart, consider the score you gave yourself on the previous exercise, and then list below what you would like to see yourself do to lead more from self-love, starting tomorrow. First, honor the things that you are already doing, such as breathing freely, eating well, meditating, or taking walks. It is critical to acknowledge and remain accountable to anything that you are already doing that helps you to be in your heart. What we are already doing from our heart is just as important as the things we want to see ourselves do more of.

Also identify a few things that you would like to do more of each day because it would allow your heart to be more fully expressed. This can be anything at all, but the idea here isn't to try and solve the entire world's problems, get to a perfect +100 for self-love, or to become the perfect leader overnight. We are simply aiming to move the needle in the right direction and in the ways that you and your heart have chosen.

Already Doing

Will Do More Of

_____   _____

_____   _____

_____   _____

_____   _____

Review your list and take a moment to consider just how good it would feel to be doing those things every day, even before jumping into emails and conquering your to-do list.

So often we hear people inquire what others would do if they had an extra hour in their day. Most people respond that they would use the time to catch up with life (e.g., sleep, work, clean, run errands). That's fine. We all have things to catch up on. However, you now have an opportunity to center on what is most relevant to your own heart where you can more fully live your life. Consider how much freer you'd be breathing, how much more in touch with yourself you would feel, how much easier it would be to perform at a high level with a whole heart.

This is the doing that needs to be done in the world. For all of you who love checking to-do boxes, check these boxes of the heart, and know that others will naturally check themselves. Above and beyond all the bullet points that your job would like for you to do, the things that you have just listed here are the ones that show you how you love yourself—that is your real work to be done. You were not designed to be your title, your salary, or your resume. You were designed to breathe freely with joy and love yourself.

This is why it is so important to honor the wisdoms that you knew were true when you were young. You actually had it right in the beginning, before it was coaxed and socialized out of you. Just as the fleeting memory of being the kickball captain on the playground years ago may remind you of just how awesome you were then, your centering self-love can give you the same mechanism to unlock the internal power that you are looking for in your life now.

It can be hard to shift based on a truth that feels so distant from where you might be in this moment, where self-love is not yet synonymous with leading well. But this is a worthy journey toward living and leading from joy, and it will forever be worth the effort.

Just keep in mind that the future of work will not require you to do more. It will require you to be more of who you already are. For those who can tap into their own self-love, this is an invitation to be free beyond the constraints and worries of vulnerability. For those who are reconnecting with self-love, it will feel good, but still, you may find it scary. It may be difficult for you to consider self-love as a sufficient mechanism for leadership at all times and in all spaces. It is necessary, you might concede, but it will take some convincing to see that it can be more than sufficient to lead a life worth living from your whole heart at all times.

You can be grateful for your degrees and credentials if you feel that those paths along your leadership journey gave you more breath and allowed you to unleash your wisdom. But for all the leaders who are exhausted from their journeys and out of breath, we honor the love that you had when you were a child, and we invite that self-love to take center stage in your leadership journey. Such are the sparks of wonderment that swirl in our souls and make new connections across silos of information, learned experiences, inner truths, and profound wisdoms to light our humanity with newfound delight. You were right when you were young. You were right to feel connected to all things and seize every challenge as a new opportunity. Now is the time to move again from that knowingness.

EXERCISE 4: Truth Be Told

In Chapter 4 we explored rules for The Brighter Side of Leadership, universal truths that govern our hearts. Yet that list is not complete if it does not cover your model of self-love, your own personal truths.

If you could go back in time and rewrite the rules of the corporate mindset and/or those of the playground from the wisdom of your inner child, what rules for leadership would you use to ensure that you could become the leader you wanted to be? What else do we all need to know to benefit from the diversity and wisdom that you bring? Use the spaces below to jot down a few of your core truths of leadership and begin to formulate your own unique leadership brand, rooted in the wisdom of your heart and inner child. If you notice any fear, anger, or jealousy underlying any of your rules, simply acknowledge that this is your brain still fighting. Your heart might have better and more complete language to offer.

_____

_____

_____

_____

Excellent! Just look at those amazing truths—so simple, so transformative! Now consider what it would look like to live and lead from those truths, every day, in everything that you do. Now that you have reengaged with your heart and unburied these wisdoms, you can't go back. You can't just ignore what you now know to be true. The only path is forward. The only way is you moving through the world radiating these truths from your heart, in joy, in all that you do.

LOVE LIGHTS THE PATH
TO LEADING WELL

We would all like to move with ease through the world, breathing freely, filled with love of self and a knowingness of our own truths. This would allow us to tap into and remain engaged with our innate wisdom at all times. We can do this, but we must first let go of the idea that we can somehow buy our way or busy ourselves to self-love and joy. Moreover, we must stop leveraging the impressive-sounding titles, power, and influence we've picked up from the corporate mindset.

In the end, it all comes down to two options: (1) pursue money and title first, self-love after, or (2) do it the other way around. It should be clear by this point what order the colonial mindset endorses and which one we suggest.

The old mindset's version leads us to believe that if we get enough power and money, we will be freed up to pursue self-love. We take it as a matter of faith that when we have the requisite title, money, responsibility, and power that we will then be able to work on our self-love and self-development interests. So we willingly put self-love on the back burner. But we already know this doesn't actually work. We have yet to meet the super-successful, wealthy person who, after a "big" career, felt inspired to finally do the work of self-love.

In fact, it's quite the opposite. We have met many people who, after very "successful" careers, realized they hated their job, hadn't done anything meaningful, and still didn't know how to love them-selves. We have met them in their critical moment, trying to jump off the hamster wheel of success as it continues to spin and spin and spin in self-loathing despair as they finally reached out for help to begin the journey of self-love. We have also met the leaders who consider it enough to be someone else's version of a leader during the week and their own version of a leader on the weekends. Though they may be able to make it through the year, we rarely see this strategy work for a lifetime.

Yet we don't have to look to others when we can look to ourselves. At the end of the day, it's a decision we each must make in our own hearts. Many of us have earned more money, gained more impressive titles, and have had more influence and more power as we've progressed through life. Yet, for nearly all of us, we now have less time, not more, to focus on our self-love and self-development. So what makes us continue to believe that this pattern will so dramatically shift? We have conflated the belief that if we are good people, we will be rewarded for eternity in heaven with another belief that if we do good work for our boss, we will be rewarded with eternal self-love. This just doesn't make sense.

Let's play it out: if it were true that those with more money and power are eventually freed to pursue self-love, we would naturally expect to see the wealthy awash in self-love. Meanwhile, those of lower socio-economic standing would be nearly devoid of it. Not only is this not the case, but if anything, it appears the opposite is true.

This is something your heart has likely known for a very long time: self-love must come first. To be fair, this can still be viewed as a matter of faith that once you've obtained a requisite level of self-love, financial success will follow.

But let's allow our hearts to do a wisdom check on that. When tapped into self-love, we are more authentic and more effective in everything we do. While this is no guarantee of grand riches, it certainly optimizes the likelihood of it. Moreover, it all but negates the alternative outcome. That is to say how can we, fueled in our own self-love, really ever fail? What does "failure" even mean in a world where we are brimming with joy? We can tell you that it does not look anything like the threat of failure the corporate mindset uses to threaten us at every turn. It doesn't look like destitution. Instead, it looks very much like learning and growth.

Not recognizing this truth has led us as a society to revere wealth and not our own transcendence. We lust for jewelry and cars rather than wisdom and oneness. As such, the value and virtue of self-love has been removed entirely from the daily doings of the workplace and the boardroom. It costs us, individually and collectively, with every non-self-love-informed business decision we make. And the irony is that it ends up costing us exactly where we were expecting to profit: our bottom lines.

LET LOVE LEAD

To ask humans to produce without self-love is like trying to turn on a light bulb missing its filament. It is like expecting a tree to grow without water. The reason why productivity, engagement, and satisfaction in work are all so low is because people are running around without the energy and wisdom they need to produce anything meaningful to their soul.

Collectively we are going out of our minds over-engineering this and that, pushing everything through the industrial complex. It's a job, we say, and it is, but at what cost? We simply can't lead when our hearts are on hold. All of our energy is disconnected from the joy necessary to empower humanity to truly evolve for the better. Younger generations get this, but the colonial mindset fights them as they try to bring a little healing to the world.

When it is safe to love yourself and you can see other people leading from their whole selves, there is a bridge. There's an open invitation to believe that you, too, can create the space you need to live and lead from your authentic leadership presence. Those who honor their own self-love inspire others to do the same. For too long we have been taught to turn away from love as a productive mechanism of leadership in the name of conformity, which is fear's nice way of saying *control*.

Resistant leaders stuck in the old mindset are threatened by the notion of people bringing their whole selves to work. They think it's dangerous. Everyone will be running around the organization with their emotions on their sleeves. It will be bedlam. And to be clear, we've literally heard this from people. It is exactly the fear-based thinking that has everyone's feelings bottled up and unresolved in the first place. And to be fair, they are right to a degree: there is a humongous number of pent-up emotions just waiting to come flooding out. But isn't that just testimony to exactly how toxic the workplace has been for so long?

Forcing people to fit into an unhealthy organizational culture is an invitation to be unwell and un-whole. This is critical because it's a perfect setup to ensure that everyone is fragmented from their own sense of self. The real irony is that this is exactly what directly dampens productivity, the one thing that companies most want. Further, when everyone is fragmented and leading from a lesser version of themselves, it's cruel and operationally futile to then try to hold people personally accountable. The corporate mindset is, in effect, constantly saying, "Be less, but do more. And eventually, once you have mastered that, we will reward you enough for you to see that, one day, you might be able to love yourself (maybe, but probably not)."

Given the state of society and all the ways in which everyone has been taught to either fight against one another or fight for their right to breathe, choosing to love yourself is the defiant act of giving yourself permission to leave the battlefield and lead from beyond the fight. The fact is that people need to overcome their differences and learn to work together for the benefit of our collective evolution. That is the point. Leading from love is the mechanism of evolution. Feel the breath in that!

LET LOVE CROSS INTERGENERATIONAL BARRIERS

Let's look at this through the lens of the generational perspective. Each new generation feels somewhat constrained and controlled by the generations before them. People also tend to get caught up in the relevance of their own struggles and fail to see how the fruits of their labor are realized in the freedoms of each new generation that follows. Instead, they hear entitlement and feel threatened by the next generation. So they fight with younger generations, the very people benefiting from the very freedoms that they fought for. They try tirelessly to convince younger people that they are not working as hard as they should, let alone as hard as the older generations had to. They treat the next generation as ingrates clamoring for an easier life when they already have it all. This is what happens to leaders when self-love is made irrelevant. We can't win for losing, and we lose even when we win.

In conversations with baby boomers who are concerned that their children have forgotten their parents' contribution, we are always struck that they cannot hear how their children being unburdened by the struggles of the past is a clear and evident win-win. To see, hear, and feel the lightness in young hearts is actually the indicator that things are, in fact, moving in the right direction. To weaponize the output of evolution gone well—usually by calling it softness, laziness, or entitlement—is to only ensure that no one wins, nothing changes, and we all stand still.

"Make America Great Again" is essentially a battle cry to never heal, to stop growing, and to succumb to the way things once were. That's certainly not the path to the "more perfect union" affirmed in the preamble of the US Constitution.

People are fearful that their way of living, struggling, and overcoming will be forgotten or diminished. But evolution always continues, as it should. It is useless to fight against it, for that's like fighting the laws of nature, the universe, and God. It's the very height of brain and ego. Instead, we need to see the world and each other through the lens of shared love and mutual commitment. To keep our hearts open to our collective growth as a nation and as individuals who love each other and ourselves.

To illuminate how this concept works in real life, we'd like to share the story of one of our coaching clients. She's a reasonably successful young entrepreneur with an entrepreneur father and corporate executive mother. In her work to understand the wisdom of her heart, she came to realize that she operates best if she can work from home in the mornings and then head into the office in the afternoons. As she runs her own business, she can do this without issue. It allows her to focus on high-level and creative aspects of running the business earlier, then more on the details later in the day, instead of clouding her brain and heart with those finer points first thing. It is her way, and it works well for her.

Yet when her choice of how she schedules her day comes up in conversation with her parents, the response is clearly split. From the entrepreneurial father, the response is typically something along the lines of "That makes sense. There are just some things you can't really do at the office. There are too many distractions there." But from her corporate executive mother, the response is more "Ugh. This generation is so entitled. Who do you think you are, rolling into the office at noon?"

Now, does this response make the mother a mean or bad person? Do we honestly think that the mother is trying to negatively impact her own daughter? Almost certainly not. What is really happening here is that the mother is fearful. She's fearful that her daughter may not be working hard enough to experience success. She's afraid that her daughter will be judged for being privileged, not hardworking enough, being lazy, or not being serious about her business. She's fearful that the way she did things may no longer be relevant to her daughter, that her daughter may not appreciate her way. She's worried that her daughter may be becoming like her dad, and not like her, or that perhaps she loves her dad more. All of that fear is coming from her brain and clearly not from her heart. So, even though she loves her daughter, the expression is not one of love—instead, it's laden with judgment.

In response to this pattern, what can we expect the daughter, our client, to do? She can try to ignore it, maybe take some space from her mother and/or simply not share as openly with her mother in the future. All reasonable options, but they all fall under the umbrella of avoidance. To remedy this situation, we must tap into the expression of her heart and call in the heart of her mother. So, we asked our client to go to her mother and simply ask what it is that she intends to accomplish when she responds in such a way. Their conversation illuminated that the mother was trying to help, in her own awkward way, but she was doing so from a place of fear, ego, and brain. And since her daughter engaged her mother with an open heart, it didn't take much to tap her back into the actual love she has for her daughter and to change the behavior entirely.

We share this story because it encapsulates so many of the concepts we've covered so far. In this anecdote we can hear (1) how the corporate mindset tries to propagate and sustain itself, (2) how ego, brain, and fear lead us to fight even those we love and who love us, (3) how, when tapped into our hearts, we might trigger others who are still in their brains, and (4) how, as we learn the truths of our heart, we must also learn to express those truths and continue moving in those truths regardless of what is said or done by those around us, even our own mothers.

This is the work of not only discovering and knowing our truths but ensuring that we continually hold to them in our daily lives so that they might guide us to be the leaders we are meant to be, even in the face of intergenerational disconnects.

LET LOVE RESTORE HUMANITY
BEYOND RACE

These patterns and truths cross many boundaries. We can also look at the same concept through a racial lens to understand how competition breeds fear in leadership and how love conquers fear.

People have been taught that different skin colors are a threat. Because of this perception, leaders compete according to one's skin color. At this point, effectively all leaders in the corporate mindset are not bringing their whole selves or their best selves to their work. They are either (1) strategizing against someone because of their skin color (i.e., racists), (2) protecting themselves because someone is threatened by their skin color (i.e., people of difference), (3) trying to sneak around the edges of corporate culture without triggering a "race war" or getting caught in the mix (i.e., politicians), or (4) masquerading at the corporate ball, like they are not part of it (i.e., most people).

Even in this oversimplification of how racism and colorism play out at work, you can clearly see that instead of operating out of love, leaders are having to spend way too much time and energy fighting against one another over something that we could all love about ourselves and each other. Have you ever seen a child engage with a person of a different color for the first time? They are fascinated! They find it new, beautiful, and magical. That is who we really are. That is the wisdom we all had as children and learned our way out of.

Some of our ancestors may have weaponized the beauty of skin color, but that certainly doesn't mean that we are obligated to embed it in everything we do. At least we don't have to be so distracted from loving ourselves when we all have the same wonderful traits: bodies that evolved various skin tones to acclimate to different climates—it's amazing! Leaders negatively impacted by oppressive work cultures that are phobic about skin color are left with little room to breathe and get good work done. Lack of self-love fosters lack of love generally, along with lack of acceptance of and openness to the wonderful variety of people and cultures inherent to the human race. Again, leaders are left out of breath and competing against one another in a battle where we all lose.

When you love yourself, it is easy to see how childish and unproductive it is to take a thing like skin color and weaponize it for hundreds of years. It becomes even more inane if you swap out skin color for any other feature of our bodies. What if round-cuticled people hated square-cuticled people, or people with large hands thought they were better than people with small hands? To even go down that brainy judgmental pathway is akin to the mental illness of body dysmorphia, as it requires an unhealthy obsession on a specific aspect of appearance. It is complete nonsense to weaponize people's bodily traits to make yourself feel better and someone else feel smaller and call that winning. It's delusional, at best.

Only by leading with and through our hearts can we tap into the wisdom that all phenotypic expressions of our genes are what enrich the soil of humanity. Understand that we can apply the same wisdom to show how it is true for every other ism you can think of: ageism, heterosexism, ableism, racism, genderism, and the list goes on and on. They are all outdated conflicts of the past that are still infused in the unspoken rules of the corporate mindset.

LET LOVE INSPIRE

Cultural differences are blessings of humanity and were never meant to be the basis for conflict. The corporate mindset is desperate to avoid conflict in the name of bottom-line success, and this compromises the culture of an organization. That is why diversity is still largely considered a burden in the corporate world and, at best, is considered merely "nice to have," far below profitability on the priority list. Again, the irony is that with true diversity, profitability naturally follows. However, this is a legacy of the colonial mindset that continues to distract us from our individual and collective evolution.

The bottom line is that every leader has the opportunity to choose their own heart as the foundation for how they live and lead. Similarly, organizations have the opportunity to build cultures that inspire the best in people and lift every heart. Both at the individual and institutional levels, people are designed to lead while breathing freely, loving themselves and others, bringing their best to the work, and creating new pathways of success. When leaders are able to show up as their whole selves, that is when they are most sustainably creative and innovative. Leaders who are able to show up more authentically with joy in their hearts can inspire an entire organization to reach new unimaginable heights.

Chapter 7

BREATHE INTO JOY

You are not the value of your work. You are the value of your heart. Both struggle and happiness exist outside of your heart. As the wisdom of our hearts now reminds us, struggle is placed upon you by those who want control above all else, and certainly above your freedom. That is their struggle, not yours.

Meanwhile, happiness has been so confused with joy that most people don't know the difference. This is important because happiness and joy are qualitatively very different.

RESILIENCE OF JOY

Happiness, just like struggle, is influenced by outside factors. Joy, on the other hand, is intrinsic and motivated from within. Happiness is a short-term and often fleeting experience. Once the outside stimulus that brings us happiness is removed, happiness goes with it. For example, if chocolate cake makes you happy, then when you eat chocolate cake, you are happy. When the piece of cake is gone, however, your momentary happiness fades.

Joy is much longer lasting and far more resilient in the face of obstacles. Yet, as we've seen, joy has been rendered irrelevant as a mechanism of personal development and empowerment. As a result, people have come to rely upon happiness to get through challenging moments, even though happiness does not really function well in that capacity. The odd result of all this is that people feel, through the fleeting nature of happiness, a false sense of strength. And they engage this strength for overcoming struggle in the given moment (e.g., "If I can still experience happiness, then I must be stronger than the fight. I'm not letting it get to me.").

However, when we understand happiness for what it is, we can see that this is nothing more than a temporary and incomplete coping mechanism. In the temporal experience of happiness that arises when a person feels charged up in the face of real-life obstacles, these feelings are fleeting. Just like when the chocolate cake is gone, so will happiness fade when the obstacle is removed or when the person finds they can't budge it.

Because happiness is fleeting, any attribution we attach to it will be fleeting as well. If we feel elated while eating cake, the elation won't last when the cake is gone. What do we do then? We either seek out more cake or we find ourselves back at square one, or worse. In other words, we continually require further external validation and motivation to endure and recover from current challenges, and to buck ourselves up for whatever comes next. Leaders who continually hop from one moment of happiness and struggle to the next often consider themselves deeply resilient. However, when we understand happiness and the false resilience it provides, we see reality for what it is. A person may seem resilient in the moment, but over a lifetime, they will almost certainly exhaust and deplete themselves traversing so many highs and the inevitable lows that follow.

> Constant fighting to overcome social ills or other people's traumas is a losing game.

Of course, there's some strength in being resilient in the moment, but the attainment of resilience for a lifetime can only be ensured by the lasting effects of a joyful heart. Depending on happiness to fuel our daily struggles just sets us up for an addiction to struggle for our dose of happiness. So it becomes clear that resilience only in the face of struggle cannot be a productive source of power or a worthy goal. Constant fighting to overcome social ills or other people's traumas is a losing game. It dampens our capacity to shine beyond the notion of struggle and truly break free from who we were forced to become to simply survive. As a result, we set the bar far too low.

We think that by being temporarily resilient through happiness we will begin to have enough breath and peace to find self-love. But we don't. Accomplishment in the name of survival is too often short lived and insufficient to empower ourselves into joy and self-love. Of course, there is honor in struggle, but the highs and lows distract us from becoming centered in our joyful selves.

A heart in joy does not say, "I celebrate my resilience!" A heart in joy says, "I celebrate my radiance!" The difference between resilience and radiance can best be described as two different sides of the same breath. One is in struggle; the other is in joy. So let's unpack what it means to radiate from one's sense of whole self.

YOUR OWN VERSION OF A LEADER

During a workshop a few years ago, a leader told us that we might be pushing too hard, that we needed to understand that not everyone wants to be a great leader. We explained that our encouragement was simply an invitation and opportunity for each of us to become our best selves. It is a choice. Why would anyone choose otherwise? Everyone wants to be some version of a better leader, right?

Stepping back, it's easier to hear that this leader was simply saying they didn't want to be a particular predefined version of a leader. That it felt like an undesired pressure or expectation. Yet what they weren't hearing is that we were inviting them only to be the best version of their own natural self. We were simply asking for more of it in a way that fuels each person's own self-love and joy.

Unfortunately, many leaders have been wounded by the constant pressure of the corporate mindset's very specific, and often unsavory, version of a leader. And from that perspective, our invitation to truly center one's self-love felt so foreign and unfamiliar that it seemed like something to be feared and fought off. If all you've ever been told in your life is that you are not doing a good enough job, then our invitation might sound like some version of "C'mon! Get your shit together! Be more yourself! It's easy! What's wrong with you?"

This is, most certainly, not that. If any of what we are sharing here feels that way to you, recognize it as an old, ingrained message pattern getting in the way. Just remember to breathe and come back into your heart and joy. When you do, you will know that every heart deserves to experience the radiance of its wisdom being expressed in the world through joy. That is the full expression of one's self-love. It can't be that we were given a heart so wise and radiant only to be fearful of shining it. It's time to stop letting old trauma or fear dim our natural, joyful light.

To be radiant in the world is to unapologetically let your heart shine with the brilliance of your own self-love and know that it is your superpower. To shine and know that you are bathed in the power of your own self-love is truly awesome. It is what we like to call "joysome." So, what we are calling forward here is not pressure linked to a singular view of what a good leader is. Instead, we are inviting you to be absolutely free to be all of you, shining your whole heart with every ounce of who you are designed to be: your joysome self.

Joy Is More Powerful than Struggle

All the ways in which we have been forced outside of our own knowingness have caused us to learn from the bottom up through the struggles of life. As a result, we have come to think that struggle is a productive mechanism for growth. It has become so normalized that many of us even find gratitude in the misfortune of someone making life difficult for us: "My parents were really hard on me, but it made me strong."

Struggle has been convoluted as the mechanism of personal growth. With only the most limited consideration for the extent of a person's trauma, struggle is regularly touted as a necessary evil in life. People tell of the most horrific things that happened to them, only to conclude that it made them better or stronger in some way. For many, it seems that the pattern of struggling and overcoming is necessary to just make progress in the game of life. In other words, if they are to move forward, it must be through struggle. Or, put another way, a good life must be a hard life.

If we choose to struggle for the rest of our lives, then it seems somewhat reasonable to have externally induced happiness to give us a break from it. However, the misuse of happiness to survive struggle is what keeps us content to keep struggling on to the next hit of happiness. This is far less effective and productive than accessing the ever-abundant reservoir of self-love and joy contained within our hearts.

THE JOYSOME HEART

Some people describe being fully in their own radiance as feeling an extension of their authenticity beyond the boundaries of their physical body in a way that invites others into their own authentic selves. This is why the power of attraction is a very real thing. This is not ego. This is not us taking up space or sucking the air out of the room. It is an offering of truly safe and sacred space to partner, co-create, and innovate.

It is the permission to be safe enough in your heart that you can authentically extend such space to the hearts of others in a way that calls forward true and authentic connection. As bell hooks once said, "The only way into really being able to connect with others, and to know how to be, is to be participating in every aspect of your life as a sacrament of love." If you want to engage in the world in a meaningful and dynamic way, then the journey requires that you become centered so deeply in your own self-love that you can ensure that you are meaningfully engaged in your heart enough to safely partner.

Imagine teams of leaders, each having done their own work to live from a place of self-love and now being able to partner from the radiance of the wisdom of their hearts. Now that is a different kind of energy to cultivate at the beginning of a project! Imagine what such a team could accomplish. Imagine the wisdom, the innovation. It would be astounding! It would be joysome! From this place, we can switch from the usual bottom-line expectations to the top line of joyful innovation, creativity, and growth in the workplace.

Consider the energy that most people bring to work. If it isn't downright toxic, it is, at best, steeped in the "happiology" mindset, endlessly seeking the next jolt of happiness to keep floating through the day. That might feel good in the moment, but it is not sustainable for the journey, let alone for anyone to authentically partner.

Let's take it out of the realm of work—let's consider romantic partnership. The same things shake out. If the partnership revolves around a happiology mindset, it will only serve as escapism from trauma as each partner bounces from happiness to struggle and back. It may feel like the relationship provides safe spaces to catch a breath, and to be fair, this is certainly better than a relationship forged in trauma, which is also all too common. Yet, in such a romantic relationship, there is little to nothing that empowers, elevates, and facilitates evolution. At best, it is a return to zero from the negative, with little that is both positive and sustainable to show for it. To be sure, it is not the powerful connection that can occur when two people are fully breathing in their whole selves, safe in their own hearts, and connecting in the shared radiance of their joy.

SELF-AFFIRMATION

For many people, radiance can feel new, different, and even awkward. To understand this, we must appreciate just how oriented to struggle we have become. We have been so well trained in the dampening of our energy that it can feel gratuitous, indulgent, or even selfish to ramp up our energies.

Those who have been to therapy for depression know what it feels like to down-spiral as one negative thought leads to another with distortion after distortion. So we must learn to end that pattern and get back to a level state, a return to neutral. Those who have gone to therapy for panic attacks know that part of the treatment is to first come to awareness that their body is not having a heart attack. Then through deep breathing exercises, they learn to relax and bring their heart rate back to normal. As kids we are often taught to count to ten before expressing anger. As healthy adults, we know what it feels like to navigate negative energies like depression, anxiety, and anger to get back to a base state, but we don't know how to harness and expand the energies of self-love.

In your own heart, positive feelings reverberate and flood your body with hormones that lift your energy with joy. This feeling is higher than happiness. It is fuller and has more depth. When we are affirmed in our own sense of self-love, we can connect with positive affirmations from previous experiences of self-love, and this energy begins to rise exponentially. For some it can even feel like a drug-induced high, but it is a natural state that comes from within. Call it joy. And because it is derived from within, it has all sorts of productive qualities that we can tap into. These experiences become data from which you can draw a more holistic understanding of who you are and always have been.

Each productive experience of self-love leads to another in a continual elevation of heart, brain, body, and spirit toward joy. This is different from the experience of happiness where the feeling of elevation begins to dissipate when an external stimulus is removed. That is the danger of trying to ride the wave of happiness from one happy moment to the next.

In self-love, the energy does not dissipate because the stimulus is you and cannot be removed. The joy we experience in self-love cannot be distracted by external triggers such as past traumas because our hearts are always right there with us. Instead of being triggered, we simply revisit the fullness of each experience of self-love. This extends like a warm halo of light, overwhelming whatever external stimuli might otherwise negatively affect our thinking. This is not dissimilar from what some call a state of inner peace.

However, when most people think of inner peace, they imagine someone sitting quietly, meditating, very Zen-like. This is more active, but the result is the same. We stay untroubled by the world outside ourselves as we feel the peace, love, and wisdom that comes from inside ourselves. This ensures that we stay in our hearts, and in doing so, we stay tapped into our own best selves. When we practice in this way, we can go even beyond inner peace to higher levels of joy.

BREATHING INTO JOY AND ONENESS

Earlier in the book, at the beginning of Chapter 4, we walked through an exercise of breathing into a state of peaceful self-love. Now we are going to leverage our breath once again to go beyond peace and into joy. This exercise is a bit trickier and can take some practice, so don't be frustrated if you don't get there right away. The real key to this exercise is to simply give yourself enough time, space, peace, and freedom to get to joy and allow for it to come whenever it arrives.

Joy Exercise

First, find a quiet place to sit. Make any adjustments you need to find a comfortable position. Some people like to lie down, but a comfortable seated position is preferred to avoid falling asleep.

Begin to breathe peacefully with long, slow, cleansing breaths. If your mind wanders, focus on your nostrils, feeling the cool air as you inhale and the warm air as you exhale. Continue following your breath until your mind settles and you begin to feel at peace. If worries, concerns, fears, or any other negative thoughts enter your mind, simply smile at them, recognize that this is the corporate mindset doing what it does, and go back to the feeling of air on your nostrils and your sense of peace.

Do this for as long as it takes until your mind fully settles down and a sense of peace prevails. When you have reached this peaceful state in mind and body, sense deeply the core of your being in your chest. See if you can feel, hear, and sense the beating of your heart. Smile to your heart and thank it for beating so rhythmically and so consistently every moment of every day since you were born.

Go deeper. Feel the energy of your body. Feel how amazing this manifestation of you is with all of its wondrous parts. Smile at all of your lovely body parts. Appreciate the awesomeness that is you, if only for the fact that you are a moving, living, breathing creature who is alive right now and able to consciously witness its own existence.

Go deeper still. Think of all that you have done with this life so far. All that you have accomplished. All the love you have shared. All the joy you have experienced. Smile in the awareness of how tremendous an impact you have already had on this universe by simply being you. This is breathing into joy. Take note of how it feels. Where in your body do you light up?

If we are able to breathe into joy, then we need only go a bit further to also discover oneness. Allow yourself to become more aware of the impact you have already had on this universe. Note how the fingerprint of your influence is indelibly marked on so much in this world. How people think differently because of you. How people have different life circumstances because of you. These can be people you had a tremendous impact on, like family or dear friends, or people you only once touched briefly, like a store clerk or someone you lent a dollar to. Note how wide and varied your impact on this world has been. Smile at the wide and varied impact you have had.

Then, holding on to that energy, also consider how much the world has impacted you and all the countless ways that many thousands of people have imprinted themselves upon you through interactions big and small. Notice that as you have imprinted on others, they have imprinted upon you. And just like the inhalation and exhalation components of your breath, one cannot exist without the other. They are inextricably linked. You are them, and they are you. You are the universe, and the universe is you. This is breathing into the joy of oneness.

The Joy of Oneness

When you experience self-love, you can become consciously aware of a feeling of oneness in both heart and brain. In some Buddhist circles, it is referred to as the awareness of "interbeing." However, to be clear, while we can cognitively understand interbeing with our brains, this is rooted in heart energy and must begin from a place of whole self and self-love. The consciousness of oneness will multiply your own sense of self-love in a way that allows you to experience your movement and progression through the world in a very connected way, with all of your senses actively engaged. It is as if you can more clearly see, hear, and feel all the ways in which other humans, animals, and nature are moving as one.

This is the experience of joy. It is much like hitting "the zone" for an artist or athlete. There is a deep alignment of one's brain, heart, body, and spirit in such a way that it allows us to experience higher states of consciousness, including oneness, interconnectedness, and interbeing with others and our environment. This higher state of connection allows us to fully access all the data that we have obtained in self-love and begin to put it into action with a level of ease that can wildly accelerate our actual real-world performance. This is what we call a "heart in action."

A heart in action is a state in which a person feels complete alignment with how they see themselves and who they are designed to be in the universe. They can feel their body moving as one in alignment with the universe, and it is all stimulated and kept on track from within their own heart. That is where the authentic power of who you are lives. And because it comes from within, you can extend it beyond any given moment and tap into it as a natural state of being that you can continuously live and lead from for a lifetime.

JOY ILLUMINATES

The beauty of joy is that even though it is completely derived from within your own heart, it has an incredibly dynamic energy that can also be shared with and experienced by others with little effort. While there is nothing more powerful than experiencing that sense of oneness with the universe, it is incredibly uplifting to share that sense of oneness with others in a way that inspires and empowers them to their own self-love and journey into joy.

Joy does not need the tools of our ego to sustain itself.

If you don't have a sense of what it means to share your inner power of joy with another heart, then perhaps you can remember when you last felt it from someone else. We all know when someone is authentically in joy. We can see it on them, even from a long distance. We can experience joy radiating beyond their energetic field and interfacing with our own. This is more than being inspired by the words of a charismatic leader. It is even greater than being able to see someone's positive aura. It is more like a powerful magnetic connection authentically connecting one heart to another, often with transformative outcomes.

The key behind joy, different from other states of positive affect, is that joy productively empowers the hearts of others to authentically connect with their own sense of self-love. The person receiving the productive power of joy does not even have to be in a conscious state of self-love to fully experience it. It is as if seeing it in someone else reminds our heart of what it already knows to be true. The truth is our heart was designed to love itself too. This is why seeing someone in joy does not trigger envy. There is no reason to be envious of something that we also have inside of us. Joy does not need the tools of our ego to sustain itself. Competition, greed, guilt, control, manipulation, titles, and money all seem like trivialities when we are in joy.

From this place, with this clarity of view, we can allow for even more space for people to comfortably stay in joy. Experiencing the radiating influence of joy helps to illuminate productive qualities that can be leveraged in others and in our own leadership.

TRANSFORMATIVE IMPACT OF JOY

One way to measure leadership is to consider how it influences others. When we say "influence," we don't mean control or manipulation but rather authentic motivation. Joyful leaders don't exert power over others, as in brain-driven leadership. Although not all brain energy is bad or evil, it can certainly be dangerous, as we've previously explored. Instead, when the mechanism of leadership is heart-driven, then we can be assured that it is authentic and good. Joy is the most authentic version of productive influence a leader can have. One heart energetically empowering another. What could possibly be more productive?

Joy eliminates the fear that corporate mindset leaders use to manipulate others in the name of motivation. Consider that parents, teachers, managers, and even CEOs don't like using fear-based tactics to motivate their kids, students, teams, and cultures. But so often, they do. Most people know in their hearts that they are doing something that is unkind, short term, and in many cases, kind of grimy. Afterward, many will reflect on how they feel bad for how they chose to lead. Personally, we have always found leading from our brains exhausting. The problem is that most of us simply don't know what else to do. "My dang kid won't eat his brussels sprouts! What else can I do but bribe or threaten him?"

Some of us have learned to use positive forms of motivation, but when they don't work, we are quick to slip back to our tried-and-true fear-based tactics. This is why joy is so important. It is a free source of motivation that not only empowers the leader experiencing it to perform at a higher level but also taps other leaders into their own joy in a way that enhances their output as well.

The transformative impact of joy is multilayered. This is because there are internal outcomes within the leader whose heart has been activated into joy, as well as external outcomes that directly affect those around them. When one person experiences joy, it directly impacts all the people around them and indirectly affects all the people around all those people, simply as a result of being inspired into their own joy.

This is not the traditional model of competition in which others feel pressured to perform. Instead, this is like watching a group of artists become inspired by each other's work. Comedians, actors, writers, and dancers all do this well because they are more readily freed into the art of what they do. They free flow and find inspiration in one another to aspire to do bigger and better jokes. They enact more meaningful scenes that convey true human emotion. They write ever greater tales of wonder. They try new dance moves that call to the hearts of others with such passion that they no longer seem to dance but are simply a body in motion, one with the universe. Such productive impact does not have to exist only in the artistic world. It can exist in meetings, on project plans, and in boardrooms. We would all be better if it existed in the workplace, not limited to the spaces that we run to again and again after work for authenticity and rediscovery of our breath.

> Most people are not present to how joy moves in them every day.

As always, we don't want you to accept this as truth just because we say so or because it sounds good. The productive impact of joy is so real that you can track it for yourself. As part of our work, we created the Joy Tracker because we realized that people were struggling to name their joy. They had never been given the time to collect or process their own experiences of joy. Joy has been reduced and bottlenecked into only what we do when we celebrate or go on vacation. As a result, most people are not present to how joy moves in them every day.

Of course, joy is present in our lives beyond the celebrations, but we tend to fail to notice. So we created a mechanism to give people the opportunity to easily track their joy each day, and you can do it too. The Joy Tracker calls people into their own personal experiences of joy while tracking who brought joy to their heart and who they shared their joy with. It also helps leaders begin to understand when joy bubbles up into the next layer of radiance so that they can make it a more regular thing. If you want to start tracking your own joy, just hop on our website at www.bigjoytheory.com/joy-tracker and sign up—it's free.

We tend to feel particularly overjoyed when leaders receive the experience of our joy in a way that inspires them to pass on their own unique brand of joy. They share stories with us of how, finally, their heart was able to productively impact the hearts of others in ways that they always knew it could. For us, it is like watching someone breathe in the full brilliance of their own heart for the very first time.

In joy, leaders find the words to finally express the wisdom of their inner child—not through fear, worry, or concern of being rejected, criticized, or ridiculed but unapologetically through their own voice of self-love. They offer their voice of joy to their families, their mentors and sponsors, their bosses, and their CEOs. And because they are speaking the language of the heart, untethered and unbothered by ego, they finally say what they have been trying to say all along. Moreover, because it is the language of the heart and not the brain, their thoughts and ideas are finally heard and received. All of that, in half the time, simply because the voice of joy is so authentic that it cuts through the chatter of fear that we used to carry in our brains.

This is the truest and most productive impact of joy. Hearts liberated beyond the constraints of the corporate mindset can tap the authentic inner smile, which the world then receives in a way that creates even more opportunity for joy to show up and do what it knows how to do. In that freedom is where so many leaders finally give their hearts permission to bring their creative flow back to the world. Within that expression of authenticity are their best ideas, most creative visions, and most transformative innovations. This is how we begin to lead with wisdom, which is the subject of Part III.

Part III

LEAD WITH WISDOM

Chapter 8

IN JOY, WE LEAD

When we choose to live and lead from our own self-love in each and every moment, we also choose joy for a lifetime. This is nothing new. It has always been true. But now you can see, hear, and feel that the unspoken rules of the corporate mindset required you to move through life in a way that kept you out of breath and steeped in conflict.

That conflict builds up various tensions and blocks in human consciousness that make it difficult to remember who we truly are in our hearts. This is why we come to overly use our egos to survive. It's also how we have come to be so fragmented and disconnected from one another.

Our way back to ourselves and each other is through joy. Joy is the mechanism that allows us to safely and securely reopen the flow of our hearts so we can live more meaningful lives connected to the power of all living things. Leaders all over the world are now talking about joy because it is finally time for people to stop fighting and return to the notion of who we are as one people.

With joy as your foundation for living and leading well, you will move through the world with a sense of wholeness in everything you do. The sensation that comes from being whole stems from being aware of who you are when you love yourself and are fully expressed in the world through joy. The final phase of the journey is to learn the true power of the wisdom of joy that can inspire the doing that you wish to see and perform in the world.

In this way, everything that you do can be motivated from a place of deep connection within yourself. It can come from a place of self-love and elevate through your heart into oneness, radiate out into the world, and empower you to move in ways that reflect your heart over your ego. This is how you can ensure that you are authentically showing up in the world with ease. That is how we offer the certainty that struggle is not required for you to grow. Struggle is not necessary for the journey of leadership. It is not an important factor in you becoming you. It is a distraction from who you truly are in your heart. This is the truth, and this is why it is so important for you to find who you are in joy.

JOY IS

Even though every leader may know joy when they experience it, joy has not been well understood as a mechanism of productive transformation or defined in a way that allows us to claim it as the power of our hearts in action. Joy is a whole-body experience. It is more than a moment. It is more than what is in your DNA. It is more than your psychological makeup. It is the energy of your soul.

As we progress from a service-based economy to one of experiences and transformation, we can consider joy the full-body immersive experience of self-love, the transformation of how we live each day. This is why joy cannot be broken into component parts. As the saying goes, "The whole is greater than the sum of its parts." Joy is greater than the sum of each unique experience of self-love. It is more than the smile that comes from within when one says, "I love myself." It is more than the experience of feeling your heart in action in any given experience. It is more than having others say that they love you for being you. It is more than others loving how you love yourself. It is all of that and so much more.

> The future will be driven by creativity, co-creation, and innovation.

Joy is the cumulative effect of you smiling with your heart because you love yourself. When joy reverberates within, it also radiates out into the world through your energy in a way that inspires every heart around you to self-love. This is why the wisdom that comes from joy is so transformative. Remember that wisdom is the product of knowledge (all that is outside of you) combined with the intuition of your heart (all that is inside of you). Your wisdom of joy is uniquely yours. And wisdom can be shared from one soul to another through heart-to-heart communication. With so many wise hearts in the world, one could be perpetually inspired by the people around them in ways that are truly transformative for everyone.

Joy as the mechanism of transformative leadership can call each leader into their own internal desire to lead from the true power of their heart, with full and complete wisdom and accountability. It cultivates a positive and productive pathway of growth and development for each heart to bring its wisdom to the world. In fact, joy cultivates space for the deep sense of connectedness we need, individually and collectively. Connectedness that can inspire us to build pathways and systems to support the future of humanity. The building blocks of the future will not and cannot be driven by the energy of our egos. The future will be driven by creativity, co-creation, and innovation. These building blocks are the true wisdoms of humanity and leveraging them now will allow us to keep up with the pace of evolution, all while breathing and smiling at the brilliance of our own hearts in action.

Therefore, joy is being called forward as a model of leadership. Once embraced, joy will become the mechanism that empowers each leader to trust and be accountable to the wisdom of their own heart. When we come together in joy, we are constantly ready to create, collaborate, and innovate in our ever-changing world. This will reshape how organizations empower their leaders and teams. In turn, it will create the space to transform education, healthcare, finance, and every other industry, from the inside out. Technology will be used to cultivate real and meaningful opportunities for us to express more joy in the world. This is the pathway that leads to the future. You choosing the wisdom of joy in your heart is critical to the whole of humanity becoming one again. Then we will work together and leave all the fighting behind us.

The future of work will not require you to do more. It will require you to be more of who you already are. Who you are is in your heart. The wisdom that it carries is your truth. The true message of your heart is expressed in the world through your joy. This is why joy is the transformative mechanism. Focus on bringing your joy to the world, and you will bring the wisdom of your whole heart to all that you do. This has always been true, but now is the time to unleash the power and brilliance of your own heart. Your joy is worth more than a moment; it is a lifetime.

LET YOUR JOY WORK FOR YOU

There are two final pivots we must make before we jump into joy completely and ensure that you have joy at the forefront of leading well. First, it is important to reiterate that joy is both the pinnacle and pathway of success, not the celebration of it. Therefore, joy can and must be leveraged as an input to, not just an output of, success.

Leaders who know how to operate from the wisdom of their own joy will be able to bring their creativity to the world, not just in one particular area of expertise but at any time and across any domain that their heart feels compelled to engage in. In this way, the silos of leadership become irrelevant. Like many artists, leaders will come to see that their joy is applicable to a wide range of modalities. An artist might study one form of painting for years and then come into their own different style that allows them to authentically express their brilliance. We call these their phases or periods, and we celebrate that. But then we don't extend the same freedom and delight to our own evolutions. Joy is that freedom. Joy is that delight. Joy is what allows you to move, guided by the wisdom of your heart, from one period to the next.

The second pivot is to understand that joy as an input has profound productive value for us as individuals and for organizations. The corporate world is just starting to understand this. A hundred years ago, if something terrible happened to you physically while at work, that was just your bad luck. Your employer had no responsibility to assist you. You were usually fired shortly thereafter as you were less capable on the assembly line or whatever the physical work you engaged in might have been. However, as industry matured, we learned to create workplaces that are more or less physically safe. We created rules about what should happen when people are hurt at work and what employers are responsible for. Certainly, you can still turn on late-night television and see countless legal ads: "Hurt at work? We can help!" But the point is that there are even laws for those lawyers to leverage to support those who are physically injured at work. We learned that physical safety was a requirement and a right to do good work.

However, most of us today do not primarily work with our bodies. Instead, we work with our minds and, most importantly, with our hearts. If you experienced a terrible but nonfatal and not cognitively debilitating calamity, and you must now use a wheelchair, for example, how much worse at your job would you really be? For most of us, the answer is, not much worse at all. And it could even provide new insightful perspectives that were previously unavailable to us. As such, we are recognizing new and more relevant forms of safety in the workplace: emotional, psychological, and even spiritual. As we continue to realize the value of making workplaces safe in this way, we must include opening work to the value of joy and self-love. When workplaces become safe spaces for open hearts, people will be freed to tap into their joy to produce the highest quality of work. Joy has the transformative power to lift people to their highest level of authentic performance. It is the only stable mechanism that can allow for every human being, each and every heart, to release their magic for the benefit of all humanity. It is the responsibility of every leader to choose joy as the foundation upon which they live and lead. It is also the responsibility of organizations to choose joy as the mechanism through which their leaders productively grow.

JOYFUL EVOLUTION

The leadership framework of joy is a cyclical progression from self-awareness to self-expression to self-efficacy, as we will explore further. This is what we mean when we say that joy is within; it is your whole heart in action. This is why it feels so good when you are fully you, because it is actually your joy radiating into the world in full brilliance. Remain fully you, and what was once a moment can become a lifetime of living and leading well.

The Cyclical Progression of Self

Joy as a model of leadership allows every leader to name and claim their own model of authentic leadership based on their own data. No longer will leaders have to rely on models set by others when they can so clearly leverage a model they already have within. No longer will leadership be about marching to the beat of someone else's drum and rule set. Leaders will be able to flow with their own internal model that they have quietly and surreptitiously been using their whole lives, despite all the challenges and struggles. Leadership in joy builds upon itself in a dynamic model we call "The Joyful Evolution of You," as shown in Figure 8.1.

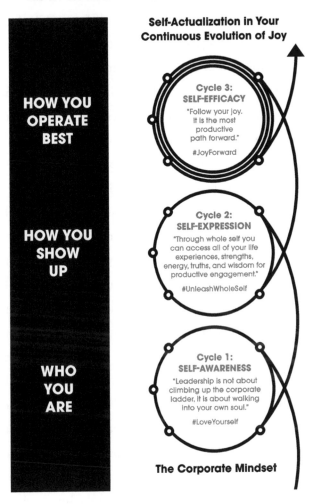

Figure 8.1

"The Joyful Evolution of You" begins at the corporate mindset, where we all start our journey working to detach ourselves from an ineffectual and oppressive rule set. From there we enter the first cycle, Self-Awareness of Joy, followed by Self-Expression of Joy, and finally Self-Efficacy of Joy, which leads us to self-actualization in our continuous evolution of joy. Note the small dots along the cycles. These are experiences of joy that further inform our self-awareness, self-expression, and self-efficacy of joy. Identifying those experiences and learning to leverage them is a critical component of your evolution and something we will discuss in more depth shortly.

We will step through the cycles of this model in greater detail, but first, to understand the entirety of this model from a high level, consider your favorite food. Whatever it may be, you likely ate it a few times before you truly recognized it as your singular favorite. You didn't eat it for the first time, jump up, and exclaim, "This is now and forever my new favorite food!" It took a few times, but steadily you became aware that it was a food you enjoyed more than other foods, until finally it took its place at the very top as your favorite. That is the awareness cycle. From there, you likely began telling people that this is your favorite food, in large part so that they will know to give it to you or help you to get it. Some people, tackily, even go so far as to adopt the food as a pseudo middle name. This is the expression cycle. Finally, if we are really serious about our favorite food, we begin to learn where to get the best, perhaps even travelling across the country or globe for the absolute best versions of our favorite food. We may learn how to make it ourselves and perfect our own recipes. This is the efficacy cycle. Throughout all of this, of course, we are eating the food, learning more, delving deeper into what we like, how to share it with others, and how to get more and better versions of it. These are the experiences of your favorite food from which you can leverage for the benefit of yet further awareness, expression, and efficacy.

So too can we engage positively and productively with our joy. But unlike the simplicity and superficiality of a favorite food, we can leverage the self-awareness, self-expression, and self-efficacy of our joy in every facet of how we live and lead.

Cycle 1: Self-Awareness of Joy

The self-awareness of joy is understanding who you are based solely on when you are your whole self, at your very best. To develop your own understanding and awareness of who you are in joy, you simply document and then analyze the data from all your experiences of being your whole self. Your data can begin from documenting your most recent experiences or your first ones. The point of this process is that it tips leaders right-side-up in their own evolution, centering them on the power and brilliance of their own hearts in action. This is the data that was rendered powerless when joy was made irrelevant to our lives and work. It is critical for each leader to reclaim this self-awareness as they work to understand who they truly are and how they lead best.

EXERCISE: Experiences of Joy

Take a few minutes and come up with ten different experiences of you operating in your whole self. These are experiences that could have lasted a few seconds or spanned many years, experiences in which you could really feel that inward-outward smile of being your very best. You may have been super productive, or you may have been relaxing on a beach somewhere. This isn't necessarily related to work, output, or outcome. This is about finding those experiences where you felt that you were 100 percent you. These are the experiences of you in your highest vibration. If a stranger watched you during this experience and it was all they knew of you, they would actually understand you pretty well, maybe better than others who have known you for years. As you recall these experiences, simply jot down a few notes or a title of each experience for your own recollection in the spaces below.

Be careful not to overthink this exercise. Give yourself time to open the space for your experiences of joy to reveal themselves to you. Just sit quietly and let them come to you. If you continue to struggle, sometimes touching base with a trusted loved one can help get the memories flowing. List as many as you'd like, but try to give space for your heart to share at least ten such experiences.

When was the first or last time you experienced joy? The time after or before that? The time after or before that?

_____

_____

_____

_____

_____

_____

_____

_____

Well done! You have completed the important work of naming your joy. This is vital, but our work is not yet done. Now go back through the list of experiences you've noted and reflect for a few moments on each. As you do, see if you can identify key themes about who you are in joy. Step back into each experience and feel your presence and energy. Were you passive or active? Were you stoic or vibrant? Were you by yourself or with people? Were you thinking or being? Write down any salient themes that come up for you as you consider each experience of joy. For each experience, try to come up with at least four to five notable themes.

After you have done this for all the experiences you listed, you should now have dozens of identified joy themes across your multiple joy experiences. The next part of this exercise is to simply go through your dozens of joy themes and see what keeps popping up. Are there any themes that revealed themselves more than once or twice? Are there notable patterns in your themes? These recurring themes are what we call your key joy themes.

Your Key Joy Themes

Look back at your experiences of joy and note any key joy themes that stand out. List your key joy themes in the spaces below. Simply breathe and open the space for your soul to be curious. Allow your truths to unbury

themselves and reveal themselves to you. There is nothing more for you to do than to simply stay present and
receptive to your joy.

_____

_____

_____

_____

_____

Okay, great work. Last step. Now that you have
reflected on the experiences and the fullness of the
leader you have already been in joy, discovered the
salient themes, and distilled those down to key joy
themes, ask yourself, "What is now true about who I am
in the world around me?" Try to encapsulate your identified key joy themes into a sentence or two that really
captures who you are and how you lead in joy.

**What is now true about who I am in the world around
me?**

_____

_____

We have tracked the responses of leaders who have completed this exercise, and the results, unsurprisingly, are absolutely breath-giving. When asked what is now true about them and the world around them, leaders say the following:

- "I am love."
- "I am safe."
- "I am whole."
- "I am full of strengths."
- "I can always touch my joy."
- "I am not what I do. I am how I do it so well."

Leaders will often share a deep knowingness that they are truly free. Whatever it is that comes from the wisdom of your heart, it will be your truth. But it is a truth that you must name, center, and honor for you to elevate into your joy as a leader, and for all of us to benefit from the wisdom of your joy.

Going back to the cyclical progression of joy, we see that as we emerge from the cycles of self-awareness, self-expression, and self-efficacy, we can ask these same questions. The exercise we just completed contains the truths that shook out from developing a deeper self-awareness of joy by revisiting previous experiences of joy. But we can do the same investigation at the culmination of any of the three cycles. "What is now true about who I am in the world around me?" is a question to reflect on, to validate your journey through a cycle and solidify its learnings so that you can hold on to them as you progress to the next cycle.

Knowing your own data on joy allows you to be accountable to your joy, today and tomorrow. It removes the day-to-day pressure and the constant stress of hoping to get to joy, one day. Instead, it gives you the information that you need to own your joy within and learn how to cultivate a life of joy where you know that you won't have to hope for anything. This goes back to the concept of joy being an input to your life but also takes it from an input just for today, or for some upcoming project, and centers it as an input for the rest of your life. With your new truth in hand, you can't go back to believing otherwise, let alone acting from those old false beliefs.

Cycle 2: Self-Expression of Joy

As we gain greater self-awareness of our joy, we naturally evolve and move into the second cycle, the self-expression of joy. Self-expression of joy is moving through the world while tapped into your whole self and allowing that sense of joy to inform who you show up as, regardless of context or surroundings. It ensures that you are outwardly communicating the truths you've cultivated through your self-awareness of joy so that not only do you know these truths, but everyone around you knows them as well.

The self-expression cycle is where we begin to understand how our newly discovered truths in self-awareness interact and are best understood by the outside world. How do you communicate who you are in joy so that others can best receive you? How do you express yourself verbally? How do other people understand and interpret your joy? What clothes do you wear? What do you start or stop doing?

To be clear, this is an exercise in understanding both language and behavior and how they authentically interact with those around us. Also, please note that we are nearly 90 percent done with this book, and this is the first time we are concerning ourselves at all with how others receive us. Until now, we have solely focused on ourselves, our hearts, and uncovering our wisdoms. This is how out of whack we have been for the oppression of the old models. But even now, we are not concerned with how others receive us such that we worry about acceptance or rejection. We focus instead on how to best present ourselves so that we are most authentically understood. Some of this can be very loving and beautiful, and some of it can be very challenging and even painful. This is the phase where you're likely to get a lot of weird looks, and possibly even hostility from those who have long misperceived you and your joy. There are perhaps people who have benefitted in some way from you being out of breath or not fully activated in your joy. These people are not likely to respond positively to this phase. But that's okay. It's exactly the work we need to do to gain clarity for ourselves and for everyone around us. Don't worry about how others respond. Your joy will carry you through.

Start by tracking your experiences of your self-expression of joy once per month, then two times per week, then three times per day, moving to four times per hour, until it becomes a continuous way of living and leading in the world. This expansion of your joy from the inside out will likely, and inherently, shift your language, appearance, and mannerisms as you stop performing and learn to exude your own authentic presence.

You will also measure your progress toward becoming fully self-expressed in your joy by measuring the fullness of your breath. Take note that when you are whole, your breath is fully engaged. As you progress from self-awareness of your joy to self-expression, you will notice a deeper and greater breath running through you. It will feel freeing; it will feel like you are breathing cleaner, crisper, healthier air with every breath. You may also feel a dampening of the excitement you used to get when you'd try to hop from happy moment to happy moment. Instead, your energy for the love of being more authentic picks you up continually. Your mood will be less up and down, and much more even, as you will no longer be falsely elevated through fleeting happiness or falsely depressed due to fleeting perceptions of failure. Many leaders report a heightened sense of ease as they move through the world, as noticed by themselves and others. There is a general calm and a sense that you are simply more you.

To help you track and reflect on your experiences and expressions of joy during this time, feel free to leverage our Joy Tracker at www.bigjoytheory.com/joy-tracker.

After giving yourself a month or two to move through the world, working to fully express yourself in your own sense of joy, again ask yourself what is now true about who you are in the world around you. What new truths have unveiled themselves as you have learned to better express your joy to the world around you?

What is now true about who I am in the world around me?

_____

_____

Following the "self-expression of joy" cycle, leaders that we have worked with tend to answer this question with responses such as these:

- "I lead from the right seat on my own bus."
- "Everyone sees and understands me and my value."
- "Joy is relevant to my authentic self-expression and performance."
- "The only thing that can keep me from fully being me is me."
- "Me first, for all the right reasons."

This is the part of the journey into joy that is truly liberating. It feels like liberation because you will finally feel free to be you, fully expressed and understood. Moreover, you will see how by being fully you, you call other people in, beyond the mundane rules of engagement, so that they can see you more clearly. Those who heed the call will see you more clearly than they ever have. Those who don't will simply be revealing more data about who they are and what they are capable or not capable of doing with you. Learning to truly self-express in your joy liberates you with such ease that it illuminates the full illusory nature of the corporate mindset and renders it a dead, useless relic of history.

Cycle 3: Self-Efficacy of Joy

The third cycle, self-efficacy of joy, is fundamentally the process of building a life that continually calls us forward into our joy. It is about surrounding ourselves with people, artifacts, processes, and behaviors that lead us to do all the things that are positive and productive for us to be in joy, stay in joy, and further manifest ever more experiences of joy in our life. It is about setting up a life such that the world bends to us and our joy, rather than a life in which we constantly try to react to the wants and needs of everyone and everything outside of us. It is a bit like the process of becoming an artist.

In this cycle, you begin to fully lead from your understanding that becoming the leader you want to be is about developing your own unique form of leadership art. As a leader, you have your own special process of creativity, co-creation, and joy. Understanding what that looks like is your self-awareness. How you express your art and your process of creating in the world is your self-expression.

From here we can now drive toward real, consistent, and prolonged innovation, the things that only you can do, that the world has never seen before, which we simply call your self-efficacy of joy.

It is in this cycle that we may be called to leave a job or a bad relationship. It is also when we may redecorate our home, move to a healthier environment, or change other fundamental aspects of how we live so that we can more safely cultivate and express our joy. The point of this third and final cycle is to build a life informed by your joy such that your joy is always centered and held sacred. Know that if you can do that, then everything else will naturally fall into place, for you and for everyone around you.

This final cycle can take a bit of time, from multiple months to even a couple of years, because it is a call to truly lead from joy in every aspect of your life. If you need to sell your house, move to a different part of the country or the world, and build your own business to live a life of fully efficacious joy, well, that might take some time to do. But typically, what we see is that right off the bat, people begin to reprioritize self-care over caring for others to ensure that they can sufficiently stay in the breath that is needed to activate the wisdom of their heart.

Leaders realign their schedules, projects, connections, and career goals with the authentic expression of their heart, now understanding what it looks and feels like for themselves, releasing the need to live and die by the bullet points of their to-do list. Instead, leaders simply wake up in joy and remain curious about how the universe will call upon them to bring the wisdom of their heart to do amazing things that day.

After you've taken sufficient time to enact these changes in your life, you should again ask yourself what is now true about who you are in the world around you. What new truths have come to light now that you have made real strides in creating a life built around your joy?

What is now true about who I am in the world around me?

_____

_____

As leaders have emerged from the "self-efficacy of joy" cycle, they have shared with us new truths such as these:

- "This is like living in a whole new world."
- "There is nothing more for me to do than to simply be."
- "Bringing my whole self to the work is the doing to be done."
- "Joy is my bottom line."
- "I am going to be just fine. I just have to keep breathing."
- "I just have to keep leading through my whole self. What I do is just what simply falls out of me from there."

In self-efficacious joy, leaders get busy living a life of joy while remaining open to continuously deepening their self-awareness and becoming even more fully self-expressed. Please remember that these are cycles—not steps, not phases of development. They do happen in a progressive order, but they are not discreet, and they are not finite, nor should they be. You will constantly deepen your self-awareness of joy as you learn to express it and as you work to build a life around it.

It is for this reason that you may have noticed in Figure 8.1 that the third cycle has multiple loops. This is because you will most consciously and continually be in cycle 3 for the rest of your life. Of course, you will continually revisit each of the three cycles, but it will feel as if you are constantly developing a more effective way of living, more in tune with your joy, even as, invariably, your joy shifts over time. It is for this reason in particular that the journey into joy is so wonderful and beautiful. It is never completed; it can always be more. You get to keep learning more and more about yourself and how you can move in this world. How joysome is that!

The journey into joy is one of never-ending self-exploration, interfacing with others, and deepening of practice. There is no destination. There is no end goal. You are to enjoy the journey itself, and that, dear leader, is why it is so fundamentally different from the other models you've been offered or compelled to use in the past. The goal is the journey. The journey is the goal.

Chapter 9

THE TANGIBLE
APPLICATIONS OF JOY

I t is now time for leaders to be defined by the fullness of their joy
within. When a leader understands who they truly are in joy, it
allows others to experience the wonderful brilliance and freedom
that comes from a heart in action. It is through joy that we can truly
understand the wisdom that each leader brings to their work and to
everything they do. When we cultivate a space that empowers our
own joy and the joy of others, we no longer have any need to worry
about what does and does not get done. We simply celebrate how,
not what, we did oh so well.

Now that we have walked through and can understand the evolution of joy in our hearts at the individual level, it is time to expand
and work the concept of joy through the heart of an organization,
from hiring to managing to promoting and even to transitioning.
What would happen if we stopped measuring work product outputs

and instead learned to measure development of whole human beings? To do so would radically shift focus from who we are "supposed to be" at work, to who we truly are as human beings, and who we are as our most productive selves.

LET JOY INFORM THE FUTURE OF WORK

The truth of the matter is that the world is changing at an increasingly rapid rate. This will require new models of work. We cannot carry the old, clunky models of the past forward. We must cultivate models that are more honorable and dynamic, more inspiring and productive.

Work performed from a place of joy at the leadership level can be replicated at the organizational level. It is a process of opening the model from the inside out. There will still be structure, but the structural frame will no longer be designed for top-down control. Instead, it will be designed to allow the heart of each leader to be more realized in a way that benefits both the individual and the organization as a whole.

It is only a matter of time before corporations as we know them fall away. The change has only just begun as institutions have emptied their buildings to allow for leaders to work from home. It is important to realize that humanity has been asking for this change for years. However, it was only during a global pandemic that organizations finally began, or were forced, to listen. They were only willing to change because of the demands of a public health crisis. They had no choice but to adapt. It could have happened years ago when the hearts of so many leaders and staff began asking for change. Regardless, now the change has begun, and smart organizations will work to promote the capacity for joy in our work-life.

> Bring joy into the industrial complex and watch it transform.

Just as you must put self-love first for your own development and the achievement of success, the same is true for teams and organizations. Imagine if not only you but everyone you worked with were tapped into the wisdom of their hearts, brimming with self-love. Can you imagine what you might achieve? Creativity and innovation will flourish in correlation to joy, along with the bottom line of revenue and profit. What may sound like a utopian concept can be a realized truth if done for all the right reasons.

Bring joy into the industrial complex and watch it transform by nature's own design. Allowing joy to inform the pathway to the future of work will require just two things: (1) the choice in each heart to lead from the foundation from one's own self-love, and (2) the opportunity to be self-expressed in joy. It is the second one that requires full accountability and partnership on behalf of the organization.

To this end, everyone will need to be seen as a leader, managers will become coaches, and everyone will have access to the support of coaching and appropriate mental health services. Teams will function more like communities, and organizations will evolve into dynamic ecosystems. This will require rewriting human resource policies and procedures to follow humanity and empower people forward; holding leaders accountable to the growth and development of their own heart; seeing "employees" as consultants bringing their expert wisdoms to the organization; and encouraging C-suite leaders to be the keepers of the shared space in a way that promotes co-creation and collaborative efforts. This is what the future of work will have to look like if humanity ever hopes to keep up with its own evolution.

This shift creates a bridge from the idea of leadership as management to the concept of empowering the heart of each leader to become more fully expressed in their work. Learning to do this for ourselves and for those around us is tremendously powerful as it recenters what truly gives us the nourishment that we all need to grow our joy. Moreover, as we continue to transition from industrial jobs to creative ones, outsource analytics to computers and leave strategy and imagination to humans, and move from providing services to offering experiences, the need for leadership to make this transition will become only more necessary. The future of work will demand it, but there is no reason why we cannot begin, and benefit, today. By definition, to innovate we must do things differently from the past.

We must think differently from the status quo. This is why nothing can be more innovative than your joy.

JOY OF HIRING

By now, you can probably intuit the difference between how you would hire someone based on their resume, hoping that they are a good fit, and how you could hire someone based on joy, knowing that they have the wisdom to take you, your team, and the entire organization to the next level. Even if you are not in the position of hiring good leaders at your organization, you can see, hear, and feel how this drastically different lens allows for your authentic leadership presence to be acknowledged and honored well beyond your resume. In fact, most of our clients will now look at their old resumes and simply laugh. They will see how meager, incomplete, and even pitiful a representation it is of who they truly are. You likely feel the same. Trust us when we tell you that the candidate sheepishly handing you their resume also feels that way.

Good fit or not, you can count on the wisdom of joy within each leader to deliver. It has already done so, many times over, when that leader is able to demonstrate a high level of self-awareness and self-expression of their joy. It is who they are; you are simply tapping into it for the benefit of the organization. Just consider that people don't commission art based on a resume. They commission art based on a portfolio so that they can experience the artist's work for themselves.

Before they ever decide to work with the artist, they already know how the artist's work moves and inspires them.

When they have been inspired in the right way, only then do they agree to commission work from the artist because they already know the wisdom and genius they will likely receive. There can be some discussion to get to a shared vision for the piece, or to clarify parameters like size, preferred colors, greater or lesser similarity to previous works, or preferred materials to be used. But the artist's process is respected for what it is. And if a technical requirement would violate the artist's process, it is worked around, negotiated, or released in the name of keeping the artist's process pure. It is not tarnished by control, lest we risk losing altogether the very artistry they bring, and thereby the reason why we are commissioning art from them in the first place.

If the artist wants to work this way or that way, we don't really care. If they create the art in the morning or the nighttime, in silence or while listening to blaring music, even if they work sober or in an altered state, it doesn't really matter much, so long as the genius of their work comes through. We don't question each brushstroke, even if we might be an amazing artist ourselves. We simply want what the artist can do when they are at their best. So, we leave it up to them how best to do that.

True leaders are artists. You, dear leader, are an artist. How would you want someone to hire you? Whatever you feel would be right and just for your heart is probably more like what would work for other hearts as well.

JOY OF MANAGING

We have talked about this before, but now it is time to truly apply a more empowerment-driven model of leadership that is not about controlling or managing leaders. Joy does not operate on management; fully self-actualized people do not need to be managed. Rather, they are ready to be empowered. However, this requires that anyone empowering someone else must also know the wisdom of their own joy.

It is critical that leaders who are given the opportunity to empower others be able to do so from the wisdom of their own heart. When empowering leaders in joy, the primary outcome we seek is for leaders to become more fully self-expressed in their joy. Failing that, what we have is a leader who knows how they can operate better, how they can provide greater value to the organization, but we, as their manager, are failing to capture that value. This gap is a failure of leadership, and it stems fundamentally from a failure to empower others into the wisdom of their own hearts and the fullness of their expression of joy. To say that this is a pervasive issue is a gross understatement.

In our research at The Big Joy Theory, we have found that one of the biggest bottlenecks for leaders is that they are simply not sufficiently self-expressed in their joy. To demonstrate this, we developed an assessment called the Joy Quotient, or JQ. The JQ was designed to help leaders understand where they are on their journey into joy, giving scores on self-awareness, self-expression, and self-efficacy of joy across a ten-point Likert scale.

To date, with hundreds of people having taken the JQ, our data shows that leaders consistently score lower on self-expression than on self-awareness or even self-efficacy of joy. On average, leaders rate 6.9 out of 10 on self-awareness, but only 5.7 out of 10 on self-expression. Self-efficacy scores, interestingly, tend to be in the middle of self-awareness and expression, with an average of 6.2 out of 10.

This speaks to the reality that many leaders experience: their capacity to be the leader they want to be, and know they can be, is highly dependent on their capacity to understand themselves and authentically show up as who they are. Put another way, they know how they lead best, but for one reason or another, they are not free to express it at work. Nonetheless, they are still finding ways to lead from their heart and from their joy, as demonstrated by their higher self-efficacy than self-expression scores. This fundamentally speaks to the power of the heart to operate in its truth despite the pressures to not fully express and to conform to expectations as mandated by a workplace not led by joy, or when working for a supervisor who does not know their own joy.

Leaders empowering others along their journey into joy can simply leverage some of the activities we have included in this book—as well as appreciative inquiry techniques and other actionable tools and methods of positive psychology—to help leaders understand who they are when they are at their best. The key to empowering another is to do so in a way that calls the leader into their own self-love. This means that it is no longer about standard performance outcomes—at least not yet. It is about a leader empowered to step into their own sense of authenticity, so much so that they begin to radiate their own sense of humanity from the inside out.

Once that occurs and their self-expression of joy is freed, then their engagement in the organization can be more effectively aligned or refined to ensure that they are given work or projects that allow their best selves to show up and do what they have always known how to do. Empowerment is about getting other leaders to identify and hone their own model of leadership to the point that they feel the power of their own joy. Once we've done that, we can rest assured that the traditional business outcomes will be readily taken care of.

JOY OF PROMOTING

When a leader consistently operates out of the wisdom of their own joy across multiple projects and key contexts within an organization, it is a great signal that they are ready to expand into other opportunities. This is not a traditional upward promotion in which leaders are elevated to the next rung on the ladder of success with a better title, salary, and so on. This is about an expansion of the radiance of a leader's wisdom into other, often wider, areas of opportunity where they may not have seen that their brilliance was even needed.

This can look like a leader who has always been good with numbers realizing that it is not just about numbers and that they are uniquely talented at tracking gaps in the data. Over time, properly empowered, they can expand the radiance of their genius from spreadsheets and accounting to quality assurance, strategy, legal, sales management, and countless other areas, inside or even outside the organization. Heck, a great gap-in-the-data tracker could even be a powerful CEO or politician given appropriate empowerment and opportunities to self-express.

Certainly, some of those promotion opportunities might come with more money, a more impressive-sounding title, or an increase in responsibility, such as the opportunity to empower other leaders into their joy, but that is not, and cannot be, the focus. We must remain focused on this individual leader's heart having greater opportunity to impact with authenticity. When we do so—and when we ensure that they can sustain their brilliance with ease while also having more opportunity to creatively collaborate with others—that is how we grow truly healthy, powerful, impactful organizations. In this way, each leader can be assured that their organization is cultivating them to be the leader that they are designed to be, the leader that they want to be, and not simply the leader that others would like for them to be.

JOY OF TRANSITIONING

Similar to the promotion of leaders, the transition of leaders into and out of the organization no longer needs to be about good or bad behavior, or about them trying to make more money elsewhere. It will not be about fit either. Instead, transitioning someone to a new team will be about exposure of one leader to others when it truly works best for everyone. It will happen for all the right reasons. This allows leaders to experience shifts in their work and how they relate to the organization through positive opportunities, not negative ones. It also ensures that ego does not needlessly creep back into the scenario and get in the way.

Trauma is also minimized as there is no need for the leader to feel re-wounded by past experiences when perhaps they were shifted due to negative occurrences. This also holds true for when it is time for a leader to transition out of the organization altogether, whether for a new opportunity or retirement. When we learn to reexamine traditional business metrics through the lens of joy—even key metrics like employee turnover or retention—we can see that the metric itself is meaningless, at least until we understand the metric within the context of why it is happening. High employee turnover for all the right reasons is wonderful. Low turnover for all the wrong reasons is terrible. High employee turnover can, in fact, even become a positively productive indicator of a healthy culture in which leaders move around for all the right reasons. It completely releases the stress of transition and the boundary lines of what it means to change and evolve in one's positionality in the organization as one evolves as a leader.

Long gone are the days when people hoped to work at the same company for their entire career. Job and career changes no longer carry the heavy significance they used to. So why do we hold the same angst about how we move around in our jobs and careers? Through the lens of joy, we can see how each move is simply another cycle in our evolution to becoming the leader we were always meant to be. As leaders of organizations, we can incorporate that same lens into how we transition others into and out of the organization, in joy, and for all the right reasons.

If joy can fundamentally change how people leave an organization, then we can see how joy truly frees the frame of leadership. In all, it allows us to create more space so that leaders can lead from their whole hearts. With this understanding, it will be important to set aside all remaining notions of who you thought you were because of your climb on the corporate ladder, or your tenure in your current role. You can leave behind notions of who you thought other leaders were or who you thought they were trying to become. No more living and dying by the resume. No more thinking that anyone has made it because of their title or diplomas. Leaders are simply to be understood by the wisdom of their heart. And it is this understanding that underlies the final exercise we have for you on this journey into joy: cultivating a joy brand for your heart.

EXERCISE: Your Joy Brand

Go back to The Cyclical Progression of Self section in Chapter 8, and review your list of key joy themes from the self-awareness cycle. Then say out loud to yourself, "Now *this* is who I am when I am in my joy!"

Do you feel that? Pretty good, right? Now we are going to lay claim to your unique joy brand so that you can carry that feeling with you at all times. This is going to be the title that you give yourself because you now know who you are in joy, and the world is ready to hear it. The way you know you have it right is when you smile from the inside out each time you hear the title that you give to your joy.

So take those experiences of joy, your key themes, and all those wonderful truths that shook out as you navigated the cycles of self-awareness, self-expression, and self-efficacy of joy. Hold all of that as much as you can in your heart, and ask yourself: what is the most succinct, comprehensive, impactful, and honest way for you to capture as much of that as you possibly can?

In just a moment we'll give you a handful of examples to get the juices flowing. But before we do, we're here to support and remind you to not let your brain get in the way. In other words, if you're inclined to reach for a thesaurus, don't. Your joy brand needs to come from the wisdom of your own heart.

If you're concerned about whether you'll ever actually introduce yourself with your joy brand, well, that's fear—that's your brain too. The key to this is to let it come to you naturally. Breathe. Stay in touch with all the truths, wisdom, and experiences of joy that you've revisited throughout this book. Let it all speak to you. You don't have to search for this. This is, in part, what we mean when we say, "Do not work for joy; let joy work for you." Stay in your joy, and the right words will come to you. We promise. Just keep breathing and let it flow.

With these guardrails in place, we now want to share with you a few selected examples of leaders who gave themselves a joy brand promotion. We want you to feel the dramatic difference that a joy brand brings, distinct from any job title you've ever had, however impressive. Next to each joy brand, we have also included how each of these leaders were formerly titled, or "formerly known as" (f.k.a.). And just in case you are wondering, yes, the vast majority of these joy brands are actually what these leaders now use as their real titles. You'll find these joy brands on their business cards and websites. You can probably even find them, right now, by searching for these wonderfully creative, insightful, and impactful joy brands on LinkedIn. So, without further ado, here are just a few of our favorites:

- The Creative Humanist (f.k.a. Executive Director)
- The Audacious Commander (f.k.a. Chief of Staff)
- EntreConnector (f.k.a. Executive Director)
- Goddess of Manifestation (f.k.a. Founder and Consultant)
- Queen of the Presentaverse (f.k.a. Speaker/Author)
- The Financial Maximizer for Women (f.k.a. Options Trader)
- Joy Maximizer (f.k.a. Executive Coach)
- Joy Hacker (f.k.a. Entrepreneurial Coach and Professor)
- Ear to the Soul Listener (f.k.a. Schoolteacher)
- Goddess of Wisdom in The Wind (f.k.a. Executive Director)
- The Heart of It All (f.k.a. Community Program Specialist)

Pretty good, yeah? Well, now it's your turn. Your joy brand is for you and no one else; it is distinctly yours. Take this opportunity to breathe deeply and identify just the right words to capture who you are when you are fully being you, completely tapped into all the wisdom in your heart, all your self-love, and all your joy.

When you have it, use the space below to capture your very own joy brand:

_____

Now go ahead and take your own joy brand promotion to heart. Once you've identified your joy brand, you can now focus on cultivating life experiences to bring your brand of joy to the world—at home, at work, in your community, and wherever you breathe. With your joy brand in hand, your life goals are less about the quarterly or annual goals of the organization you work for and more about how many times per day, week, month, quarter, and year you can show up in your authentic leadership presence and rock your joy!

To tell you the real joy of it all, leaders who lead from their joy simply track how many times they rock their joy brand each day. They know that if they do that, everything else will fall into place. To track your joy, you can simply develop your own annual, quarterly, monthly, weekly, or daily goals for how many times you would like to show up in joy or with your joy brand centered. If you want help, again, we have our Joy Tracker to help you at www.bigjoytheory .com/joy-tracker. Either way, we look forward to calling you into the best of who you are in joy and seeing the wisdom of your heart manifest in this world.

Chapter 10

EMPOWER THE
FUTURE WITH JOY

Empowerment leadership derives from the understanding that we can best understand a person's motivations through their desire to be whole and authentically self-expressed in the world. It sits at the intersection of authentic leadership and well-being and is fueled by the productive power of joy. Empowerment leadership inspires leaders to bring their best selves to each and every moment, regardless of context, industry, phase of development, expertise, or whatever factors or obstacles have been keeping them from being their best self in the present moment. It necessitates that we all know who we are as leaders and how we lead during times of challenge, change, transformation, growth, and opportunity.

There is nothing to manage and everyone to empower.

Empowering leaders through joy lifts the constraints of management. It not only creates space for reintegration of each leader's heart in the understanding of who they are as a leader, but it does so in a way that heals leadership blocks while simultaneously driving accountability for each leader to develop, hone, and engage through their own model of leading well. Leaders establish meaning and derive deep connection through the power of joy in their hearts. They achieve impact through joy's radiating influence. Creativity, co-creation, and innovation are what naturally fall out of leaders who are empowered to lead from whole self. Therefore, there is nothing to manage and everyone to empower.

Just as you came to this book, and came to this work, when you are ready, so too will your workplace be ready. It cannot be forced, and it cannot be put on a timeline. But just as for any truly great leader, leadership can be modeled and lived. You now have your joy brand, so go out there and live it. In doing so, you can attract others to do the same, including those you work with and the people you surround yourself with. This is the power of the radiating influence of joy, and this is what you must hold to, in faith, to ensure its transmission from you to the next person, and, in time, to all who encounter your orbit. This is how we can grow and develop a model of joy-based leadership to become a team or organizational norm. Never by force, but always with the power of joy shining the light on the opportunity for something better.

When we consider what it means to lead through joy, we need

to understand that we must first live into our own joy. In doing so, we model and reflect the power of joy and free others to put joy and self-love first in their lives. The results of this can be simply astounding as we:

1. empower our own self-love;
2. empower those we love;
3. empower those we love to work with; and then finally,
4. empower the world with joy.

HEART PERFORMANCE OUTCOMES

Empowerment leadership allows leaders to measure success in accordance with what matters most to the performance of their hearts. It could be the quality of the foods they eat, the work they engage in, the friends and colleagues they keep, and the health of their family unit. Not from a place of critique about how they perform against some external standard but from a place of account-ability to ensure they are living and leading in a way that allows them to fuel their own sense of self-love to ever-higher levels of performance.

Performance indicators for empowerment leadership are heart-centered, such as "What percentage of leaders felt their heart smile back at them today?" or "Ninety-plus days since last decision made from fear." This is what joy in action at scale looks like. This is what cultivates the space for real innovation, co-creation, and productivity in life and in business.

Having a culture of joy ensures that the hearts of leaders will be ready to engage with authentic ingenuity when the opportunities arise. This is the real success organizations so desperately seek and can't attain through obsolete corporate mindset thinking. Revenues, profits, and margins all seem so silly from this perspective, but all of them are so much more readily obtained when we stop pursuing them directly while wearing blinders to all other things. Instead, simply empower people to be the leaders that they want to be in their hearts. It will be a true wonderment and delight to see what leaders grounded in whole self will end up doing with all that joy!

So we invite you, dear leader, now that you have come this far to the final pages of this joy manifesto, to bring this model to your own heart and to all of those around you. Learn to live in your joy, not only for yourself but for those you love, care for, and work with. Allow your years of experience, domain knowledge, and expertise to meld with the truths of your heart, informed by your self-love and joy, to create true innovations for the betterment of all humanity.

INNOVATION FUELED BY JOY

Consider the obvious domains that are historically plagued by corporate mindset thinking: major industries that have tremendous impact on our daily lives in the fields of healthcare, finance, education, and high tech. Perhaps you work in such a domain and understand just how deeply the corporate mindset has woven itself into the fabric of your industry. You've seen how it operates with lethargic growth and development in the single-minded pursuit of quarterly profits and glowing shareholder reports.

For example, what would a healthcare system look like if it were centered in the joy and self-love of everyone involved, from patients to technicians, nurses to doctors, environmental services personnel to chief medical officers? What might education look like if it were centered in the joy and self-love of students, teachers, administrators, families, and communities? What might policies at the local and national level look like if joy was accounted for, even just a little bit?

This is what we invite you to consider: true innovation and entre-preneurship, fueled by joy and self-love in ways that the corporate mindset could never dream of. Freed from the shackles of deficit-oriented, comparative critique, and the status quo, and fueled by your own breath, self-love, heart-informed truths, and joy, what can you do for this world? How can we all benefit from the overflow of your self-transcendence?

Consider these questions as you continue forever forward on your journey into joy. Let each and every rule of the old mindset fall away in your own life and work so that you can create real and meaningful impact in this world, in the ways that only you, in your joy, can. This is the calling that naturally comes to you when you are fully activated in your joy and entirely engaged in your evolution.

And should you ever find yourself needing assistance in your evolution beyond what we have shared here, we invite you to joyfully reach out to us through our website, www.bigjoytheory.com, or email us at joy@bigjoytheory.com. Until then, we wish you nothing but love and light in your journey and send you our grace and gratitude for the wonders that lie ahead in your evolution.

RESOURCES

There are no new ideas. We recognize that all of our thoughts are just combinations and permutations of those that have come before us. So we would like to recognize and thank all the wonderful thinkers and contributors who have influenced us and without whose collective wisdom this book would never have been possible. There are countless others, most notably our loved ones and chosen family, but here are a few of the concrete materials we can point to that have informed the wisdom within this book.

Black, Jax, & Yogev, Tomer. (2017). *Unlock the Corporate Mindset.* CreateSpace.

Desmond, Matthew. (2019). In Order to Understand the Brutality of American Capitalism, You Have to Start on the Plantation. *The New York Times Magazine.* https://nytimes.com/interactive/2019/08/14/magazine/slavery-capitalism

Fisher, Cynthia D. (2010). Happiness at Work. *International Journal of Management Reviews*, 12(4), 384-412. https://doi.org/10.1111/j.1468-2370.2009.00270.x

Fromm, Erich. (1956). *The Art of Loving*. Harper & Brothers.

Liu, Alex. (2019). Making Joy a Priority at Work. *Harvard Business Review*. https://hbr.org/2019/07/making-joy-a-priority-at-work

McGrath, Rita Gunther. (2014). Management's Three Eras: A Brief History. *Harvard Business Review*. https://hbr.org/2014/07/managements-three -eras-a-brief-history

Rosenberg, Morris. (1965). *Rosenberg Self-Esteem Scale*. APA PsycTests.

Rosenthal, Caitlin C. (2018). How Slavery Inspired Modern Business Management. *Boston Review*. https://bostonreview.net/articles/caitlin-c -rosenthal-accounting-slavery-excerpt/

van der Kolk, Bessel (2014). *The Body Keeps the Score: Brain, Mind, and Body in the Healing of Trauma*. Viking.

Lightning Source UK Ltd.
Milton Keynes UK
UKHW022200031022
409877UK00009B/309/J